52
Weeks
of Fun
Family
Service

52 Weeks of Fun Family Service

MERRILEE BOYACK

DESERET
BOOK

SALT LAKE CITY, UTAH

DESERET BOOK is a registered trademark of Deseret Book Company.

Visit us at DeseretBook.com

Library of Congress Cataloging-in-Publication Data

Boyack, Merrilee Browne.
  52 weeks of fun family service / Merrilee Boyack.
    p.   cm.
  ISBN 978-1-59038-848-8 (pbk.)
  1. Family home evenings (Mormon Church) 2. Mormon families.
I. Title. II. Title: Fifty-two weeks of fun family service.
  BX8643.F3B69 2007
  248.4'893—dc22   2007042789

Printed in the United States of America
R. R. Donnelley and Sons, Crawfordsville, IN

10   9   8   7   6   5   4   3   2   1

To the sweet children of Africa being served by Mothers Without Borders. Founded by Kathy Headlee, Mothers Without Borders cares for orphaned and vulnerable children in Africa, Romania, Guatemala, India, Nepal, Ecuador, and Bolivia. Part of the proceeds from this book will be donated to Mothers Without Borders to support their work. For more information, go to www.motherswithoutborders.org.

Also to the men in my life: Steve, Connor, Brennan, Parker, and Tanner. It has been a joy to serve by your sides and to learn to love together.

Contents

Contents

Contents

AcKNoWLedgMeNtS

No book is written without significant influence from others. I'd like to thank my husband, Steve, who has been such a wonderful partner in teaching our children to serve and has been of unfailing support to me.

I also must acknowledge the influence of my dear daddy. He was one of the most charitable people I've ever known. He taught me to notice everyone. I owe my testimony of service to him. He has passed on to the other side of the veil now, and all I can say is I hope they were ready! I'm sure he is very busy loving everyone there.

Thank you to Kathy Headlee, the founder of Mothers Without Borders, who has taught me so much about the Atonement and true charity. She is a visionary woman who has held the lamp for me to see and I thank her and admire her for her dedication to the children of the world.

I also appreciate all of the support from Chris Schoebinger and the staff at Deseret Book, who have given me so many opportunities and have been so great to work with.

PART ONE

Introduction

CHAPTER 1

The "Why?" of Family Service— Changing Lives

"Why?"

Children ask that question incessantly.

And answering that question is important.

So let's begin by answering two "whys" about this book:

1. Why did I write this book? and,

2. Why is its topic so important?

The answer to the first question came during a recent conversation I had with a group of friends. They were discussing our family's reputation for being actively involved in community service. As I pondered their comments, I responded by saying, "If I'd been more aware and known what opportunities were available, I would have started a lot earlier and done a lot more."

Bingo. A light went on in my head, and I was filled with a desire to share with other families a framework and list of ideas for getting their families involved in service sooner rather than later.

The answer to the second question—why is service so important?— becomes obvious when you think about what service does to combat a number of problems that crop up in family life.

Picture this, if you will: A mom and dad are discussing their children.

"They're constantly fighting!" says the mother in exasperation. "They're so greedy—it's always 'me, me, me!'"

"I'm concerned that they're so lazy. It seems like they just sit around and watch TV and play video games," says the father. "Don't they take life seriously?"

"I know what you mean. They're just so selfish. I worry about whether they're even developing testimonies at all," answers the mom. "Is it too much to ask that they simply share and think about someone other than themselves?"

Sound familiar? If this is you, my friend, then today is your lucky day! All of your problems will be solved—and you don't even have to throw in the ginsu knives or make three easy payments! Family service can change your family dramatically. And it will help your children become generous, charitable, hardworking, creative, faithful, and virtually every other good thing you can think of!

Children naturally begin their lives as very egocentric beings. This helps them survive. They are small and concerned with who will take care of them, feed them, and clothe them. As they get older, they gain an increasing awareness of the world around them and—hopefully—begin to change and lose that self-centeredness. We can help them move through the process more quickly if we are aware of this natural progression.

To help them through the process, we teach and train in the home, but we must also deal with what goes on *outside* the home—namely, a society that is obsessed with materialism and self-absorption, and a culture that constantly demands "more" and "better."

I went to Africa in the fall of 2006 to do humanitarian work. When I returned just prior to the holidays, I was overwhelmed with the American culture surrounding me. Just walking into a store was difficult. It was incredible to compare the unbelievable displays of goods with what I had experienced in Africa.

At the time, the Wii and PS3 were new on the market, and parents nationwide were standing in long lines for hours to drop from $250 to $600 on getting one for their kids. An employed man in Zambia was making only $200 in a year. The contrast was startling.

Equally startling was the realization that many of these parents were standing in line because they believed this new, high-tech contraption would make their kids happy. Parents today feel tremendous pressure—even compulsion, if you will—to make their kids happy. Many, in an effort to boost their children's self-esteem, have adopted the approach that they must make their children constantly happy in order to be good parents.

Presiding Bishop H. David Burton discussed this dilemma in an October 2004 general conference address:

"Parents who have been successful in acquiring more often have a difficult time saying no to the demands of overindulged children. Their children run the risk of not learning important values like hard work, delayed gratification, honesty, and compassion. Affluent parents can and do raise well-adjusted, loving, and value-centered children, but the struggle to set limits, make do with less, and avoid the pitfalls of 'more, more, more' has never been more difficult. It is hard to say no to more when you can afford to say yes.

"Parents are rightfully anxious about the future. It is difficult to say no to more sports equipment, electronics, lessons, clothes, team participation, et cetera, when parents believe more will help children thrive in an increasingly competitive world. Young people seem to want more, partly because there is infinitely more to catch their eye. The American Academy of Pediatrics estimated that American children see more than 40,000 commercials a year.

"Fewer and fewer parents ask their children to do chores around the house because they think they are already overwhelmed by social and academic pressures. But children devoid of responsibilities risk never learning that every individual can be of service and that life has meaning beyond their own happiness" ("More Holiness Give Me," *Ensign,* November 2004, 98).

So how do we combat this? How do we help our children learn selflessness? I believe that *family* service is the key. And the blessings it unlocks are many. Here are five:

FAMILY SERVICE IS KEY

When most people think of "service projects," what usually comes to mind is a group of Boy Scouts toiling away cleaning up a widow's property. Or perhaps the Relief Society sisters dutifully making quilts for LDS Humanitarian Services. But do you think of families? Do you think of *your* family? The most important place service can occur is within our own families. It is in the home that we can teach service on more than an occasional "project" basis.

This book is designed to help you with that process. It will give you ideas and suggestions for making service an integral part of your family experience. It will also help you make that service fun! Service can be a way to truly experience joy in your family.

Throughout my adult life, I have met many people who are amazing contributors. They are involved, dynamic, and sensitive to others' needs. They are making a difference in the world.

We all know some of these people as well: the guy at work who is organizing teams to go to Mexico and build homes for the poor; the woman at church who is leading a political group to protect traditional marriage; the senior gentleman who makes hundreds of wooden toys to donate to children in Africa; the young woman who has organized a group in her school district to promote chastity and self-esteem. We are aware of what they're doing and are amazed by it.

And for virtually every one of these people, there is a common characteristic. As you get to know them, you ask a question: "How did you start?" or "What made you the way you are?" Usually, that question is answered in the same way: "Well, when I was a child, I had a wonderful experience . . ." The person will then tell you, with shining eyes, about an experience from his childhood where he participated in some service and had his heart and life forever changed. Almost to a person, these individuals will testify of what I call their "transforming life experience." Virtually every person I've ever met who was deeply committed to service has had this transforming experience in their youth. And, very often, these service experiences took place within their families.

In my own life, it was making climbing toys as a family for a young handicapped boy in our community. I was about nine or ten and I will never forget how I felt when we dropped them off on his snow-covered porch and ran and hid. Those squeals of joy have rung in my ears for decades.

President Thomas S. Monson has spoken repeatedly of experiences in his childhood where he learned love, caring, and sharing, with the story of

Billy being a prime example. President Monson relates his story: "We undertook a project to save nickels and dimes for what was to be a gigantic party. Sister Gertsch [his Sunday School teacher] kept a careful record of our progress. As boys and girls with typical appetites, we converted in our minds the monetary totals to cakes, cookies, pies, and ice cream. This was to be a glorious occasion—the biggest party ever. Never before had any of our teachers even suggested a social event like this one was going to be."

Then the class learned "that the mother of one of our classmates had passed away. We thought of our own mothers and how much they meant to us. We felt sorrow for Billy Devenport in his great loss."

That Sunday Sister Gertsch taught the children a truth expressed by Jesus: "It is more blessed to give than to receive" (Acts 20:35). As she concluded her lesson, "Lucy Gertsch commented on the economic situation of Billy's family. These were depression times; money was scarce. With a twinkle in her eyes, she asked, 'How would you like to follow this teaching of the Lord? How would you feel about taking your party fund and, as a class, giving it to the Devenports as an expression of our love?' The decision was unanimous. We counted very carefully each penny and placed the total sum in a large envelope.

"Ever shall I remember the tiny band walking those three city blocks, entering Billy's home, greeting him, his brother, sisters, and father. Noticeably absent was his mother. Always I shall treasure the tears which glistened in the eyes of each one present as the white envelope containing our precious party fund passed from the delicate hand of our teacher to the needy hand of a grief-stricken father. We fairly skipped our way back to the chapel. Our hearts were lighter than they had ever been, our joy more full, our understanding more profound. This simple act of kindness welded us together as one. We learned through our own experience that indeed it is more blessed to give than to receive" (Thomas S. Monson, "An Attitude of Gratitude," *Ensign*, February 2000, 2).

No wonder that President Monson was called as a bishop at a very young age and cared for the numerous widows who lived in his ward—in fact, cared for them all throughout their lives.

Experiences like these can be transforming; they can occur within your own family and set a powerful precedent that forever shapes the future of your children—leading them on a path of love and devotion.

SERVICE HELPS PARENTS TEACH CHILDREN TO BECOME DISCIPLES OF CHRIST

As parents, it is our responsibility—indeed, our quest—to teach our children not to just believe in Christ but to be his *disciples* as well. This is our primary quest in our eternal parenting. It's important to help our children gain testimonies of the truthfulness of the gospel, the prophet, the Book of Mormon, and so on. We rejoice when our children believe in Christ. But our eternal goal as parents—the results of which bring even greater joy—is to help our children become committed disciples of their Savior.

In teaching our children to be like Jesus, we can point to his example of a lifetime—in fact, an eternity—of service to others. As we work as parents and families on becoming like Christ, we can do the things he did by serving our brothers and sisters.

The Lord tells us how in 3 Nephi 27:21: "Verily, verily, I say unto you, this is my gospel; and ye know the things that ye must do in my church;

for the works which ye have seen me do that shall ye also do; for that which ye have seen me do even that shall ye do."

In Mosiah 4, King Benjamin teaches his people what they should do as parents and as a people:

"And ye will not suffer your children that they go hungry, or naked; neither will ye suffer that they transgress the laws of God, and fight and quarrel one with another, and serve the devil, who is the master of sin, or who is the evil spirit which hath been spoken of by our fathers, he being an enemy to all righteousness.

"But ye will teach them to walk in the ways of truth and soberness; *ye will teach them to love one another, and to serve one another.*

"And also, *ye yourselves* will succor those that stand in need of your succor; ye will administer of your substance unto him that standeth in need; and ye will not suffer that the beggar putteth up his petition to you in vain, and turn him out to perish.

"Perhaps thou shalt say: The man has brought upon himself his misery; therefore I will stay my hand, and will not give unto him of my food, nor impart unto him of my substance that he may not suffer, for his punishments are just—

"But I say unto you, O man, whosoever doeth this the same hath great cause to repent; and except he repenteth of that which he hath done he perisheth forever, and hath no interest in the kingdom of God.

"For behold, are we not all beggars? Do we not all depend upon the same Being, even God, for all the substance which we have, for both food and raiment, and for gold, and for silver, and for all the riches which we have of every kind?

"And behold, even at this time, ye have been calling on his name, and begging for a remission of your sins. And has he suffered that ye have begged in vain? Nay; he has poured out his Spirit upon you, and has caused that your hearts should be filled with joy, and has caused that your mouths should be stopped that ye could not find utterance, so exceedingly great was your joy.

"And now, if God, who has created you, on whom you are dependent for your lives and for all that ye have and are, doth grant unto you whatsoever ye ask that is right, in faith, believing that ye shall receive, O then, how ye ought to impart of the substance that ye have one to another.

"And if ye judge the man who putteth up his petition to you for your substance that he perish not, and condemn him, how much more just will be your condemnation for withholding your substance, which doth not belong to you but to God, to whom also your life belongeth; and yet ye put up no petition, nor repent of the thing which thou hast done.

"I say unto you, wo be unto that man, for his substance shall perish with him; and now, I say these things unto those who are rich as pertaining to the things of this world.

"And again, I say unto the poor, ye who have not and yet have sufficient, that ye remain from day to day; I mean all you who deny the beggar, because ye have not; I would that ye say in your hearts that: I give not because I have not, but if I had I would give.

"And now, if ye say this in your hearts ye remain guiltless, otherwise ye are condemned; and your condemnation is just for ye covet that which ye have not received.

"And now, for the sake of these things which I have spoken unto you— that is, for the sake of retaining a remission of your sins from day to day, that ye may walk guiltless before God—I would that ye should impart of your substance to the poor, every man according to that which he hath, such as feeding the hungry, clothing the naked, visiting the sick and administering to their relief, both spiritually and temporally, according to their wants.

"And see that all these things are done in wisdom and order; for it is not requisite that a man should run faster than he has strength. And again, it is expedient that he should be diligent, that thereby he might win the prize; therefore, all things must be done in order" (vv. 14–27).

This is wise counsel to all of us and illustrates the importance of service in our quest for discipleship. It also clearly states our duty to teach our children to serve.

THE BEST WAY IS THROUGH EXPERIENCE

Elder Henry B. Eyring tells the story of a morning when he and his wife were rushing around getting ready for the day. He asked his wife what he could do to help, and she replied that it would be helpful if he made the bed, which he did. He comments: "It was such a small thing that I'm sure it doesn't sound very impressive to you, and it probably wasn't very impressive to her either. . . . But as I did that simple little thing, I felt something that I've felt before. When I gave of my time in a way I thought the Savior would want me to for my wife, not only did my love for her increase—I also felt *his* love for her.

"I promise you that *if you'll use your gifts to serve someone else, you'll feel the Lord's love for that person. You'll also feel his love for you*" (*To Draw Closer to God,* 87–88; emphasis added).

As I read this, I realized what those wonderful feelings were that I had been feeling as I served. I was feeling the love of the Savior for those I served and I was feeling a wash of that love from him returned to me. No wonder it felt great!

FOR SOME DIFFICULT CHILDREN, THIS SERVICE WILL HELP SAVE THEM

Another reason why this topic is so important is my son Brennan. Brennan is my second son, and (if he'll excuse me for saying so) he was a challenging child to raise. Okay, he was a prickly kid that tested his parents' abilities (and patience!) on a daily basis. When he was a young boy, my husband and I had many discussions about how to reach out to him. Our primary concern was how to help Brennan feel the Spirit. We realized that he was very different from his older brother and that what worked for Connor was not working for Brennan. We pondered and prayed over the matter and watched Brennan carefully to see what worked. Our prayers were answered when we discovered that the primary way Brennan felt the Spirit was through service to others.

Although Brennan was not very kind to his own family sometimes, he was extraordinarily kind to others—particularly those who were vulnerable. He loved the elderly. He adored animals. He was tender and kind to the physically and mentally challenged. This child who was struggling with the self-discipline to do his homework and projects in school was loving his teacher-intern class, where he taught special-ed high school students. Here was a strapping, tall, handsome, high school student who loved working with special-needs students—and they adored him. It's no surprise that he is now majoring in special education in college.

For some children, the primary way they feel the Spirit is through service to others. It is crucial that we foster these experiences for them. For Brennan, we would suggest that he go next door and help our wheelchair-bound neighbor. (To this day I truly believe God sent her to live by us for Brennan—and for her.) Or we would take him over to help his grandparents.

These children are also often the ones who need to feel the Spirit the most. For some reason, they struggle to feel loved by the Lord, as well as by others. They have an inner turmoil that can sometimes make them feel unlovable. And yet they desperately want to feel loved! As we set up experiences and opportunities for service, many of these children will feel their Savior's love—they'll feel it for the person they're serving, and they'll feel His love for themselves as well.

In fact, these experiences serving others will help *most* children feel the Spirit in a very intense and personal way. We all feel good when we serve others. We feel wonderful feelings of love and charity. These experiences can help transform our children and help them gain firm testimonies of the reality of their Savior and the plan of salvation. Their personal participation in service can sometimes be the one link between them and their path to exaltation. Its importance cannot be overstated.

SERVICE CAN HELP CHILDREN DISCOVER WHO THEY REALLY ARE

Finally, service helps children grow and develop into who they really are. All of our children have gifts, talents, and abilities from their birth and which they develop over their lives. We know that these children are valiant sons and daughters of God. Participating in service will help them truly get in touch with the greatness of their spirits. They will develop those gifts, talents, and abilities even further as they take advantage of service opportunities.

They will discover and learn for themselves that we are all brothers and sisters. They will experience this at a very real level. Aubrey, a volunteer with Mothers Without Borders, commented as she volunteered in Africa with her sister and brother-in-law, "I just love these little kids. They're my little brothers and sisters and I love them. I don't want to leave."

That sums up the whole purpose of this book—to help you know how to do family service in a planned way.

We spend many years trying to teach our children about the Savior and the importance of following his example of loving and serving our brothers and sisters, and we wonder if it is getting through to them. Let me share one personal experience that illustrates how service can foster discipleship to the core.

For years our family had been involved in service in various forms. As my own life progressed, I found myself drawn to helping the children in Africa and found a way to do that through Mothers Without Borders, a charity devoted to helping orphaned and vulnerable children throughout the world and primarily in Africa. I traveled to Zambia and Zimbabwe in the fall of 2006 to work for three weeks on various programs there.

When I came home, I shared my pictures and experiences with my family. My sons all wanted to go to Africa immediately; but Connor (25) and Brennan (21) just knew they were going to go the next year and began to plan.

Brennan went to Zambia for the entire summer, and Connor went with one of our volunteer teams for three weeks, together with my sister Andrea.

I've never been more proud of my sons. When asked why they were going to Africa, Connor and Brennan said, "We're going to change the world." And they knew they could and would.

They fell in love with the people and the children and the country. And they were touched in return. Let me share with you Connor's comments on the experience:

"My brother Brennan headed to Zambia a couple months before I arrived to work on the new land for the summer. About a week after my arrival, I asked him to tell me the main lesson he had learned during his time in Zambia.

"His response: 'Christ-like love.'

"Throughout my trip I encountered numerous examples and demonstrations of the love of this people. It amazed me constantly. My realist mind kept trying to figure out how a people so destitute, so impoverished, so victimized, could love so much.

"Perhaps the answer lies in the scriptures, where we see numerous examples of humble people having a greater capacity to love the Lord and His children. Why is it that temporal possessions and material prosperity tend to diminish our willingness and potential to love? It seems evident that living a life of temporal penury creates a natural dependency upon God.

"The people demonstrated their love so openly. I was amazed at how each day I was greeted as if I hadn't seen the person in years, when in fact I was with them a day or two previous. Each reunion was celebrated with hugs and laughter and sincere appreciation for friendship and the shared love.

"It was amazing to be in an environment where you are loved without judgment, without guile, without hidden intentions or masked opinions.

I was loved sincerely by these people who understood true brotherhood. They know that we're all God's children, and they treat you as such.

"It's odd being surrounded by unfeigned love for several weeks and then returning to a culture that in many cases is lacking in this department. Is it possible to truly love God and His children when we live affluent lives of luxury? Can we effectively mourn with those who mourn when we have no cause to mourn of our own? Can we empathize with a brother dying of AIDS and living on $2 a day when we are healthy and wealthy?

"I will never forget the inherent love that the great people of Zambia possess. They are an inspiration, and in every case I learned more from them than any of them learned from me. My return on this trip was far greater than any paltry investment I made. I will strive to be more like my brothers and sisters who truly know what it is to possess and manifest Christlike love."

It was remarkable to watch these young men volunteer their time and money to be disciples of Christ. A lifetime of service had led them to this experience, which I'm sure will be the first of many.

Linda McCullough Moore teaches her kids to set aside some of their money to purchase an annual holiday gift. At the end of the year, they count up the money they've saved and pull out a stack of catalogs to search for the perfect gift. Included in the stack of typical toy, clothing, and game catalogs are a handful of charity catalogs. Linda recalls what happened during one of their early family conversations about finding a gift: "Well, we can buy a Sega Genesis [video game system] or we can buy a goat for a village," she announced to the children.

With much excitement, her children decided to buy the goat, which they named Sega Genesis I. Over the years that followed they bought two goats and a cow for other villages. Why do they do this? Because, says Linda, "We need to teach our children that every person on the globe is more alike than different. We need to tell them that we are blessed with a great bounty we can share, that we can make a difference. Children are practical. We fear that they will worry and feel sad when shown the world's greatest needs, but much more often their response is action. They love to help. People in need are helped, human bonds are forged, children grow up with hearts more giving and more open. And every family should know the joy of owning its very own cow" ("Generous Hearts," *Family Circle,* April 1, 2005).

I urge you to do the same. Teach your children that we are all brothers and sisters and are very alike. Let them be helpers in this world. Show them how to open their hearts and be more giving. They will learn that each one of us, even a young child, can make a difference in the world.

To quote my life's motto, which I "borrowed" from Mahatma Gandhi, "You must be the change you wish to see in the world."

We can be.

CHAPTER 2

The "What?" and "How?" of Family Service—Growing, Developing, and Having Fun!

There are incredible benefits to doing service as a family. The growth and development of the children and the family as a whole will be tremendous. Here is a short list of the blessings that can come to you and your family as you participate in family service:

• It makes you feel great! Nothing can compare to the rewarding feelings that come to each of you as you serve together.

• Your children will learn at an early age that the world does not revolve around them. What parent wouldn't want that? They are exposed to major, serious issues in the lives of others, and they develop a global awareness very early that other people and their problems are important. This will provide wonderful perspective regarding their own lives and problems. An example of this is my niece Leah, who comes from a very financially successful family. When she was growing up, her family would make sack lunches for the homeless and drive downtown to hand them out. She says, "It definitely opened my eyes and I realized there were a lot of people out there who didn't have homes. It helped me see that at a young age."

• Your kids will learn to value and appreciate what they have. You can tell service is working when your child is thanking the Lord for her pillow. Blessings over food become much more sincere as children realize that not everyone has food every day like they do.

• You and your children will become less obsessed by things. My nephew Jason grew up in a Christian home and says, "We went on a mission as a family for three years in the West Indies. We took care of the needy there. One gentleman in particular I remember had no legs. We'd take him to church every week and then out to lunch. I was eight years old. The biggest impact on my life was making me aware of my surroundings. We are very blessed to have everything we could ever want and more. There are so many people in the world who don't know where their next meal is going to come from. We were the only white family on the island, but there was no color. No one cared and we didn't care. Everybody was a person." Jason and his wife will be going to Haiti next year to do service with the hungry children there, and they plan on going to Africa to help build orphanages. He has two little girls and wants to teach them how blessed they are.

• It will build confidence in family members. As family members get involved in talking to others, organizing, and using their skills and talents, they will have increased self-esteem and confidence to handle many situations.

I watched two young girls helping their father serve food at a community event. It was such a joy to see these small girls boldly taking charge and talking to the adults. Amazing confidence in such young ones!

• Your children will learn to share! In fact, we've found that as we've become aware of needs throughout the world, our children have been very generous—and this extends to those around them (yes, even their brothers!).

My friend Jenny grew up in a family that chose a needy family to "adopt" each year at Christmastime. To find this adoptive family, Jenny's family would ask the Lord in prayer to guide them to the family they should assist. Throughout the year they would save money in a jar or envelope. The children of the family were encouraged to donate part of their savings or allowance for a needy child. They would then show up on Christmas Eve with a big ham and presents for the family. Rather than buying a big gift for their own children, the parents would buy a big gift for the needy family. Then, on Christmas morning, they would gather to talk about their service and the joy it brought to the other family. Jenny has continued this tradition with her own little family. She says, "I want to teach my kids, especially in this day and age when they get handed whatever they want, that not everyone has everything they need. And you don't need to keep up with everyone else. The blessings you get are worth it. It's not about the presents or what you get. We need to think about those families who don't have everything."

• You'll have a chance to share the talents you already have. Musical abilities, artistic abilities, speaking abilities can all be used and shared with others to bless their lives and your own.

• You'll learn new things. Your children will have new experiences and learn all kinds of things that are new and different.

• Family service is the opportunity to learn and develop new skills and talents. Family members will develop abilities to organize, create, and lead at much greater levels than ever before.

• Family service will increase family unity and identity.

• It will promote the sharing of your family values. The parents will have wonderful opportunities to teach about love, patience, persistence, charity, hope, faith, honesty, hard work, and many, many more important values. And these values will be taught by experience—meaning they will sink deeply into your child's soul.

• You'll meet new people and make new friends. When my son Brennan returned from Zambia after a summer of service, I asked him, "Who was your best friend there?"

"Oh, I just loved Fred!" he replied. I was surprised because Fred is a forty-five-year-old African man who is the branch president of the Lusaka Branch in Zambia. It was thrilling to hear him talk about all of his friendships with various Zambians and how deeply they loved one another.

• As the family works together, you'll gain deeper respect and greater love for each other.

• You'll have the coolest stories to share with others!

• The family members will feel proud of who they are and how they've helped.

• Children will get a much better perspective of their lives, problems, and how they fit in God's plan. They'll have a greater understanding of the plan of salvation. Understanding that we are all brothers and sisters will become real to them.

• Your family will have amazing discussions about important and serious issues. The children will gain understanding and be exposed to global issues that will cause them to think and ponder.

• You'll have a blast! Doing service together is incredibly fun.

This is just a short list. After participating in family service, you will be able to add many, many blessings to this list.

Isn't a little time and a little effort worth it? These are tremendous gifts we can give our children if we will commit ourselves.

Sounds great, but how?

STEP 1: DEVELOP A FAMILY CULTURE OF SERVICE

The first step, indeed the entire purpose of this book, is to help your family make the decision to be a family that serves. This decision can lead to developing an entire family culture of service. Let me tell you about a few families who have done just this.

Kathy Headlee, founder of Mothers Without Borders, described her family's culture of service. Her father had gone to China to interview the founder of Project Concern International. He brought back many pictures of children and families who had escaped communist China and were living in boats and dark alleyways. Kathy was about nine years old at the time and recalls, "I remember seeing all these pictures and realizing how real this was. . . . And I kept thinking that we needed to *do* something about this." That day the light went on, and she began to see. Her family quickly became involved in great humanitarian work. Today her entire extended family has had many, many experiences serving on both a local and global level. It's now no surprise to learn that she continues to travel the world helping orphaned and vulnerable children and that each of her children is involved in serving throughout the world in various ways.

My sister Andrea has developed a similar culture of service in her own family. One of the principles she has taught her children as they serve is to be friendly and talk to everyone. In fact, it's become rather humorous because everywhere they go, the family members talk to everyone they meet—from the bus driver to the waitress to the homeless man—and it makes for long family outings! Her family has also had many service opportunities that span everything from feeding the homeless to assisting those suffering from serious illnesses. And now all of her children and their children are involved in serving others in a major way.

Serving together and participating in service projects together does much to build unity among family members. I've seen many families have this become part of their family identity. The Rosen family supports a local childcare center. The Fry family is known for their support of trails and nature preserves. The Havilland family loves Mexico and participates in regular building projects. The Boyack family is known for their dedication to and involvement in Scouting and community service. Each family, through their service together, has grown in family unity and identity.

As your family develops a culture of serving, then, this new culture will unite and strengthen family members, building wonderful connections of love and memory.

And you'll have lots of fun together! I have many hilarious memories from my own family's service over the years. Fun images come to mind: my dad helping us tie a quilt (having never done it in his life) and needing to wear a headlamp so he could see what he was doing; the children emptying the pantry of all the food they hated to be donated to a food bank (can we say canned pumpkin, pearl onions, etc.?) and their reaction when I asked them how excited they would be to open a bag with this stuff in it (they wrinkled their noses and said, "Euuwww!" and then promptly went after all the good stuff to donate); the boys running down a hill with black garbage bags flying behind them as we went to clean a park together; the family sorting through bags and boxes of toys that kept appearing on the porch to be donated to the homeless (watching three teenaged boys playing with all the dolls was priceless).

There are also memories that warm my heart. When the Cedar Wildfires swept through our community in southern California, I watched my family respond in a way that still makes me misty-eyed just thinking about it. Brennan, who was seventeen at the time, immediately volunteered to go help his friends evacuate. He called me an hour later at the evacuation center, where I had gone to help. "Mom!" he said, "you'll never believe it. Andrew and I just saved six houses!"

"What?" I asked in alarm.

"Yeah, we're over here fighting fires!" he said breathlessly.

"How do the firefighters feel about that?" I asked.

"Mom, there are no firefighters here. Andrew and I have a garbage can filled with water in his truck and we're going house to house using their hoses and saving the homes that people have evacuated."

I must admit that I felt a momentary wave of panic as I thought of my son facing the wall of fire approaching our city. And then calm came over me. I knew that he had been taught and trained for this day. He was an Eagle Scout who had badges in firefighting training, fire safety, lifesaving, first aid, and survival. And above all—he was a Boyack. Boyacks serve. And serve he did. So I said a heartfelt mother-prayer on his behalf and told him to be careful.

He and his buddy called all their friends, and dozens of young men rallied and saved dozens of homes. For months there were letters to the editor in our local newspaper saying, "I don't know who those young men were, but thank you for saving our home." Brennan's whole life was profoundly affected as well. And my husband and I have never been more proud of our son.

In the meantime, our sons Parker and Tanner lasted all of an hour at home and then begged to come to the evacuation center to help. Together, we spent the next four days helping evacuees and people who had lost everything in the fire. I could ask those boys to do anything—and they would, always working tirelessly. They were incredibly happy to help others.

Our entire family worked together for the next several months to raise money for the fire victims and gather food, clothing, and furniture. Working together as a family, side by side, for many, many hours doing good and serving together was priceless. The memories are glorious. And if you ask our sons they'll say, "Well, of course, we're Boyacks and Boyacks serve others." That statement is priceless.

I interviewed many families in preparation for this book, and I was stunned at the results. I would ask them what service they did either in their family or in the family they grew up in as a child. After a while, I realized that virtually all of them were telling me only about service during the holidays. So I began to ask what service they did as a family *outside* of the holidays. The response was surprising. I would say only about 25 percent did something as a family at the holidays to serve others. And less than 5 percent did service at other times. And you could hear the surprise in their voice as they realized what they were telling me: "That's weird. . . . We should do more. I can't think of anything else we're doing. Boy, we need to change that."

Little wonder that those families who had developed a family culture of service stuck out! They had completely transformed their families and were doing amazing things.

But I was also struck at the power of one event. Person after person could relate one event from their youth that had impacted their lives into adulthood. So even if you only do something small or even just once to start out, it will bless the lives of your children and initiate or perpetuate a culture inclined to serve one another.

STEP 2: START WITH THE EXAMPLE OF PARENTS

Once you decide to develop a family culture of service, the next step is to set a parental example.

In my family's case, it was my daddy, Roger J. Browne Jr., who set an impressive example for us. Daddy was involved in the PTA and the Chamber of Commerce, he was president of the school board, and he devoted fifty years of service to the Boy Scouts. He was an amazingly charitable man. In his elderly years, my mom would have to call the charities to tell them to quit asking him for clothing donations because he would clean out his closet—and she was tired of buying new clothes! But because of his devotion to others, all of his children, grandchildren, and now great-grandchildren are actively involved in various ways of giving service around the world.

My friend Dan Brenner followed the example of his mother, Carol, who was a lifetime volunteer with our local Rotary Club. Now Dan is involved in the Rotary and his church and brings his young daughters to participate. Three generations of serving because of a dedicated parent.

Jennifer relates that her mother was a single mother of three girls. There was a needy family in their ward who wanted to move to Utah and they didn't have a way to get there. Jennifer's mother called a big family meeting and discussed it and asked the girls if they would help this family. "We went and cleaned our old van all out and filled it with goodies for them and let them borrow it for their trip. This has always stuck with me. That she was willing to do that as a single mom was huge." Jennifer and all of her sisters have followed their mother's example of service.

STEP 3: CREATE AWARENESS AND EXPOSURE TO LOCAL AND GLOBAL ISSUES OF NEED

A third, huge component of this process is teaching your children to *see.* Too many of us spend much of our lives not looking. We don't see the poor; we don't see the hungry; we don't see the needs. If we do see, we sometimes look away because it's uncomfortable. We might see a homeless beggar and look away, afraid or worried about what he'll do with any money we give him.

But as we teach our children to become disciples of Christ and as we help them experience service, we will be teaching them the importance of not looking away. Encourage your children to *see* the needy, to *see* the poor, and to *see* the needs. Once their eyes are opened, they can then respond. They can serve. And they can then be true disciples of Christ.

It's interesting to watch children who have been taught to truly look at the world around them. They begin to see all kinds of things. And they express a desire to do something about what they see. They have very different perceptions of their place in the world and of the world in general. These children are very lively! They have definite opinions and ideas. And they are constantly asking "Why?"

In our family, I have noticed that our sons have become far more aware as we've worked on this concept. But as they see things, they'll say, "*We* need to *do* something about this!" It has been a challenge. For some reason, they think our family can change the world! I don't know where they got that idea. . . .

CHAPTER 3

WHere to Start and What to Do Next

I'm sure you're wondering, "Where do we start? This feels a bit over-whelming!"

START AT HOME

Start where it's easiest—at home! You can begin by encouraging the children to do secret favors for their siblings (we called them secret pixies) or to help Grandma and Grandpa with yard work or household chores. That's where my sister-in-law Linda started. She says, "Mom and Dad always took us up to work on a grave of one of our ancestors on Memorial Day. We would clean it up and fix it up and leave flowers. We would always go help our grandparents while we were growing up and now we do that with our children. It totally binds you as a family to take care of each other. It creates quite a love."

You can encourage your children to help each other with their chores. Make this into a fun game! And give them lots of opportunities to help Daddy and Mommy. You can then teach and train them that service feels good and makes people happy.

EXPAND TO THE COMMUNITY

Next, you can expand to the community. Begin with your local community, doing small things, and then build outward. My friend Eileen, who also has four sons, shared with me a service they gave to their neighborhood: "We put all our boys in the back of the truck and went and visited all our neighbors. Then we put together a neighborhood directory, listing all the kids and everything and printed them up. We then all put on our pilgrim hats [it was then Thanksgiving time] and went around and delivered them. It really brought the neighborhood together for years." What a unique service this family did that blessed the families in their own neighborhood.

My friend Dana related, "My dad loved to sing and he loved for us to sing. He played the guitar and we'd go sing at nursing homes—much to our embarrassment. But it makes you more compassionate and aware. I've taken my children to go visit the seniors every week and took the baby and they loved it."

You can participate in formal community events or do small projects on your own.

INVOLVE EXTENDED FAMILY

Once you're on a roll, consider expanding your family service to your entire extended family. As you involve grandparents, aunts, uncles, and cousins, the impact on your family will grow. One of my son's treasured pictures is of the family working on a quilt to help with his Eagle project. He was making quilts to go to orphan-headed households in Africa, and his grandma and granddad had come to help. Granddad was eighty-five and had never tied a quilt in his life. But there he was with his headlamp to help his grandson. A treasured memory.

You could even set up your own "Family Foundation." This doesn't have to be a large, formal foundation in the legal and tax sense. It can be an organization of your extended family to coordinate service activities among all family members. You can pool your fund-raising and maximize the impact of your donated dollars.

You can schedule service projects as part of family reunions or holiday get-togethers. Imagine how wonderful it would be to make hundreds of book bags to send out into the world from your extended family!

You can have a chairman to organize the entire family in family service. News from each family's service activities can be shared via newsletters or e-mails to inspire other members of the extended family. The possibilities are endless!

INCORPORATING SERVICE INTO THE FAMILY

You can incorporate family service into your family in a variety of ways. Any way you do it will be a blessing to your children.

Set up family home evening experiences to teach kindness, charity, and compassion. The children will be thrilled to have actual experiences to share and discuss. During these activities, talk about the Savior and connect what you are doing to him and to the gospel.

Bear your testimony often! The Spirit will then have an opportunity to witness to your children's hearts the truth of your words. Your testimony can be very brief but heartfelt. These words will touch your children deeply and leave lasting lessons.

Finally, make it fun! Play games, dance, sing, create, whistle, dress up—

whatever it takes! Make the entire experience so much fun for the children that it becomes irresistible. Not all projects will be fun—some should be very serious—but wherever possible, have fun along the way

HELPFUL POINTS

Before you begin, let me share with you some general points to consider as you start a lifetime of family service.

Plan well. Nothing can kill a project faster than inadequate planning. Involve the children in the planning as much as possible. They will develop wonderful organizational skills as a result and have great ideas.

Make the projects as hands-on as possible. Actions speak louder than words. Children learn by seeing and experiencing. There is a big difference between Mom and Dad springing for the money and Maria doing chores to earn the money and then donating it. Making things and then actually taking them to donate is very different from just having Mom drop them off.

Involve family members as much as possible. Even little Suzie who is three can hold a sign or sing. Have the entire family participate in any way they can. Let them do service *with* you. Don't just talk about it. Then you'll really have the full impact. As parents model this type of behavior, they are beginning a tradition of love and compassion that can be passed on from one generation to the next.

Make the experience real. This applies to donating as well. Use pictures and stories to make this experience very real to the family.

Build a rhythm of success. To begin with, try simple projects first (they're bound to be successful) and build from there.

Follow your children's cues. Do what interests the family and kids. If your children want to do international work, start there. If they want to do environmental work, that's a great place to begin.

Get permission. If your family is interested in working on a volunteer project, get permission from the recipient(s) and from city, town, county, church, school, or other officials and/or organizations, if necessary, before you begin a project. They'll be thrilled and can give you helpful information to make your service project more successful. Always call them first!

Watch for growth opportunities. Let your children lead! Let them plan. Let them organize. Let them speak. You can even use service projects that are designed to meet the needs of your child (Need to overcome shyness? Need to feel gratitude? Need to work on sharing?) and tailor them to fit!

Model good behavior. Talk about how wonderful it feels to make a difference in the world. Let your children see you volunteering and participating. Talk about the work of others and how much you admire them.

Be safe. Always be aware of safety issues. Young children need careful supervision. Some activities require safety equipment. Make sure you attend to this important detail with every project.

Reinforce the process. Part of the family experience is the conversations that occur before, during, and after the service activity. Be sure to talk about things! Talk about why you're doing this project. Encourage your children to discuss how they feel about the issues involved. After the project is finished, talk about how they feel, what they learned, what contribution was made. Developing charity is a process of becoming. Talking about and reinforcing that process is crucial.

You can declare this to be a "Service Year" for your family and do one of these activities every week. Or you can do one project a month, picking and choosing those you are most interested in. Use this book as a resource in helping your children participate in service as a family. At the end of the book is a list of Web sites that will be very helpful to you as well.

Invite other families to participate with you. Inviting neighbors, fellow Church members, or extended family from time to time can add a fun dimension to any of these activities.

I highly recommend that you do at least some of the fund-raisers that are listed—even though they can be challenging activities. Children need to learn that sometimes donating money is one of the most important things we can do to help people throughout the world. Do not shield them from that reality. Teach your children that it's sometimes better to donate money for a village to buy a sewing machine and fabric than to inundate them with used clothing and put the seamstresses and fabric makers out of business! Having experience with fund-raising will help them be more charitably minded and will help them face needs in the future. You'll be surprised how fearless kids can be!

If you would like to receive an electronic version of the list of family service projects covered in the book, send an e-mail to Merrilee Browne Boyack at maboyack@gmail.com or reach me through my Web site at Boyacks.com/Merrilee.

BE SENSITIVE TO THE SPIRIT AND IT WILL GUIDE YOU AS A FAMILY

People often ask "What should we do?" and "Where do we start?" I would say, start with Heavenly Father. I testify that the Spirit will guide you as parents and your family to those things that will bless you and be marvelous opportunities for you to serve. Listen. Be patient. Be brave. And you will be guided.

And remember one other thing: it is all about love. All of this. It's all about love. Loving our children. Loving our brothers and sisters, wherever they are. We merely need to follow our Savior's call: "A new commandment I give unto you, That ye love one another; as I have loved you, that ye also love one another. By this shall all men know that ye are my disciples, if ye have love one to another" (John 13:34–35).

PART TWO

52 Weeks of
Family Service Projects

WEEK 1

THaNK YoU WeeK

"You are good. But it is not enough just to be good. You must be good for something. You must contribute good to the world. The world must be a better place for your presence. And the good that is in you must be spread to others."

—*President Gordon B. Hinckley*

Collect a big pile of thank you notes and some colorful pens. Or even better—make your own notes! You'll also need address lists and stamps. Bring everything to the table and have family members write thank you notes to important people in their lives. Don't forget to include the following: teachers (Primary, YM/YW, Sunday School, school), leaders, the bishop, home teachers, visiting teachers, the mailman, the hairdresser, the baby-sitter, you name it! It's good to discuss as a family what to say before you write, as children sometimes get stuck. Talk about all the words that can be used to say thank you and perhaps write the words on a paper and post them where all can see.

Notes can be mailed or hand-delivered. Just make sure they're delivered during your "Thank You Week" or they can get lost.

MODIFICATIONS

Young children: Have younger children color a picture, then write a simple thank you note at the bottom.

Teens: For a different type of note, teens can transfer to the computer a digital image of themselves with the person they are thanking. Then they can print out a sheet with the picture on the top of the page (in full color) and write the note on the bottom of the page. They may want to include close friends on their thanking list.

FAMILY DISCUSSION STARTERS

Think about all the people who help you in a normal week. What would your life be like if they weren't there?

How do you feel when people say "thank you" to you?

How do you feel when you do something hard and nobody notices or says "thank you"?

What are different ways you can show someone you appreciate them?

FAMILY HOME EVENING IDEAS

Song: "Thanks to Our Father," *Children's Songbook,* 20.

Story: Discuss the story of the ten lepers in Luke 17.

Talk: Study President Marion G. Romney's talk, "Gratitude and Thanksgiving," *Ensign,* November 1982, 49–50.

Treat: Make Rice Krispies treats and form them into letters to make the words "Thank You." As family members eat the treats, have them say something they are thankful for that starts with the letter they are eating: "I'm eating the letter *t* and I'm thankful for my toes because without them I'd fall over!"

Activity: Start a "Thankful Tree." On the side of your refrigerator (a.k.a. "The Family Command Center") or in another prominent location, put up a large tree trunk made of brown paper. Cut out leaves and fruit shapes from colored paper. Hand out a few to the family and have them write down the names of people or blessings they are thankful for. Tape the leaves on the tree. Leave the rest in a basket and encourage family members to keep adding to the tree through the week. You can invite people visiting your home to add their "thanks" as well. At the end of the week, discuss how blessed the family is.

Recycling Week

"Be anxiously engaged in a good cause, and do many things of [your] own free will, and bring to pass much righteousness."

—*Doctrine and Covenants 58:27*

Prepare ahead by making a flyer to notify your friends and neighbors that you'll be collecting their aluminum cans and bottles. Tell them you are donating the proceeds to a charity. Ask them to leave their cans and bottles on their front porches or in another convenient location and tell them the time of pickup. This will speed up your collection!

Meet as a family and decide how you will donate the money. Recommendation: Habitat for Humanity. ("Habitat for Humanity International is a nonprofit, ecumenical Christian housing ministry. HFHI seeks to eliminate poverty housing and homelessness from the world, and to make decent shelter a matter of conscience and action." See https://www.habitat.org.)

Pick a day to go through your neighborhood collecting the cans and bottles your neighbors have gathered. You might want to use some brightly colored paper to print out short notes thanking them for their contributions. Print several notes per page, cut into strips, and leave the notes on their doors.

Back at home, sort the cans and bottles and bag them. Have the entire family go to the recycling center together to turn them in. After collecting the money from your donation, have the family write a letter to the charity, thanking them for their good work. Include a check or money order made payable to the charity.

This project can extend beyond one week. Just be sure to communicate clearly to your friends and neighbors the details of the collection time, day, and location.

MODIFICATIONS

Young children: Have young children use their wagons to help collect. Watch for sharp edges on the cans, and be careful if you're collecting glass.

Teens: Teens love to drive, so expand your route and give them the keys! You can also have them research the charity you've chosen on the Internet and make a family report.

FAMILY DISCUSSION STARTERS

Why is it important to recycle?

What things can we do to recycle?

What can we do to take care of the earth and our environment?

Why did we pick this charity?

What other things can we do to support this charity?

FAMILY HOME EVENING IDEAS

Song: "My Heavenly Father Loves Me," *Children's Songbook,* 228.

Story: Discuss the story of the Creation in Moses 2.

Talk: Study Elder Joe J. Christensen's talk, "Rearing Children in a Polluted Environment," *Ensign,* November 1993, 11–13.

Treat: Make sugar cookies and blue and green frosting and have the children make their own "earth" cookies.

Activity: Set up a recycling can and see how much the family can collect for recycling during the week.

Visit your local recycling center and learn about recycling efforts in your community.

Extended: You can contact the charity to which you donated and see if the family can support them in other ways. For example, families can sign up to help build a house in your local community with Habitat for Humanity.

WEEK 3

Make a Quilt

"If you can't feed a hundred people, then feed just one."
—*Mother Teresa*

True story: Our second son, Brennan, decided to make quilts for households headed by orphans in Africa who had no blankets or quilts to sleep on. It was quite a sight to see Scouts and their male leaders quilting away! They did a great job, and many quilts were sent off to the other side of the world to be used by children living on their own. Quilts bring love! This was his way of sending long-distance hugs.

For this project, have the family decide where or to whom you will donate the quilt. Suggestions include a foster care shelter; lap quilts for a nursing home; twin quilts to Deseret Industries, LDS Humanitarian Services, Mothers Without Borders, or another similar charity. Each charity's Web site will provide contact numbers and/or directions for how and where to donate quilts.

Ahead of time, purchase or locate items you'll need:

- Two sheets of the same size (wash and dry them)
- Batting of the same size (it's best to use one solid piece and not smaller pieces)
- One skein yarn that will contrast with the fabric

- Needles with big eyes—quilting or tapestry needles work well
- Scissors
- Large tacks
- Straight pins or a washable marking pen
- Yardstick
- Quilting frames, or four long boards with clamps

Note: If you've never made a quilt, it might be easier to invite a sister or family in your ward that has experience with quilting and can help you.

Have the family assemble the quilt. Lay out the bottom sheet wrong side up. Lay the batting on top—make sure it is fully stretched out. Lay the top sheet on, right side up. You now have a quilt sandwich! Have the whole family pick it up and begin to tack it to the quilting frame. Make sure the tacks go through all three layers of the quilt. Secure the frame with clamps so that the quilt is tightly stretched.

The quilt then needs to be marked at regular intervals using the yardstick and the washable pen or straight pins. Intervals should be no greater than three inches apart and laid out in a grid. It's easier if you use a sheet that is plaid or checkered or that has a regular pattern you can use to mark the intervals.

Thread the needles with yarn. (We prefer using double yarn, meaning you double the one strand so you are actually tying with two strands, but you can decide how you want to do it.) Teach everyone how to make a square knot ("right over left and left over right makes a knot that's neat and tight"), and begin quilting! An experienced quilter can teach you how to tie the knots as you go if you want. Remind everyone to always pull the needles through all three layers and to leave enough yarn after each knot to make a one to one-and-a-half-inch tail.

Have the youngest child be the "checker" and crawl underneath the quilt to make sure there are no knots or bunches of yarn—just don't poke them when they're under there!

When you've completed several rows, unclamp the end, roll up the quilt on the board, stretch the quilt again, and reclamp.

Gently show children how to correct mistakes. Remember, they're learning, so be patient.

While you're working on the quilt, discuss where it's going and how it will help.

When the tying is finished, you can either have the family learn how to hand-sew the edges (it's easiest to fold the top over the bottom) or ask an experienced friend to finish the quilt for you.

You can make more than one quilt! Have the entire family sign it in the corner with permanent marker.

MODIFICATIONS

Young children: Have young children be checkers or yarn-cutters, and help in any way they can. When it's finished, have them sign the quilt in the corner with a permanent marker.

Teens: Have teens research the charity online to check on delivery options. They can also pick out the fabric and yarn.

FAMILY DISCUSSION STARTERS

What would it be like to have to sleep with no blankets or pillows? How many people in the world are in that situation?

How do you feel at night when you snuggle in your bed with a warm quilt or blanket?

How does the Holy Ghost help us feel comforted?

How is the Atonement like a quilt? (It provides us with love, warmth, covering for our sins, and so on.)

FAMILY HOME EVENING IDEAS

Song: "Have I Done Any Good?" *Hymns,* no. 223.

Story: Discuss the story in Sister Margaret D. Nadauld's talk listed below. Talk about a time in your life when you felt comforted by Heavenly Father.

Talk: Study Margaret D. Nadauld's talk, "A Comforter, a Guide, a Testifier," *Ensign,* May 2001, 90–92.

Treat: Make brownies and frost with different colors to look like your quilt.

Activity: Have the entire family sit on a rug. Pretend the rug is a magic carpet and that you're flying all over the world. Sing as you fly! Have children call out places to stop; they can hop off and role-play that they are comforting someone they see. Have them visit different countries and think of different things they can do to bring comfort. Hop back on the "magic carpet" and fly some more!

Sing to Seniors

"When we do the best that we can, we never know what miracle is wrought in our life, or in the life of another."

—*Helen Keller*

Ahead of time, make an appointment with a nursing home or senior care center for your family to come sing. If you plan on using a piano, make sure the center has one. If it does not, bring a keyboard, guitar, or electronic recording.

Before you go, sit down as a family and decide what songs you are going to sing. Practice together several times. You should also practice who is going to stand where and how the music will be handled. You can have a family member play the piano (or bring a keyboard if necessary) or you can play a CD or tape with the music on it. If you're using a CD, prepare it in advance so it contains the songs you want in the order you want to prevent fumbling around between songs.

You can have fun with this and use costumes, small dance routines, and so on. Don't forget to practice!

On the day of the event, call in the morning to confirm the time and location.

Before you go, discuss with the children what some of the elderly people they meet may be like so that they are not nervous about any medical or mental conditions they might encounter. If you are concerned about a particular child's reaction, take that child to the center a few days in advance so he or she can get used to it and not be disruptive on the performing day.

Remember to bring music, CDs, players, extension cords, props, costumes, or anything else you will need. Arrive a little bit early so that you will have time to set up and can help bring in the seniors if necessary.

Remind the family that the most important thing to do during your visit is to radiate love and good cheer. They don't have to be great singers. Tell them how much the seniors will appreciate them just for being there and visiting them.

Introduce everyone when you begin (big nametags are helpful). During the performance, avoid really loud noises, as they may startle some seniors. Speak slowly and clearly in between numbers.

Afterward, visit and talk to the seniors who have come. Help the children learn how to interact with them; but don't expect more than the child is comfortable with if this is his or her first time doing this. Remember, seniors like to be touched—patted, hugged, and so on. Just be gentle and loving

MODIFICATIONS

Young children: Have young children color a picture to introduce the song or have pictures to hold during the song. Be aware that your children may be nervous, so do not leave them alone.

Teens: Have teens prepare a list of things they want to discuss with the seniors. Their first date, their first car, their favorite music, etc., are all fun to talk about.

FAMILY DISCUSSION STARTERS

What do you think it's like to grow old?

What sorts of things have these seniors lived through? (Talk about the World Wars, the Depression, inventions, etc.)

What would make a senior citizen happy?

FAMILY HOME EVENING IDEAS

Song: "O My Father," *Hymns,* no. 292.

Story: Discuss a story about your grandparents.

Talk: Study Elder Dallin H. Oaks's talk, "'Honour Thy Father and Thy Mother,'" *Ensign,* May 1991, 14–17.

Treat: Make a family recipe that has been handed down from previous generations.

Activity: Play charades, with family members acting out events from your family's history—write up brief descriptions of the events on slips of paper for family members to pick from a hat. Include events from your immediate family. They can be funny, such as "When Grandma lost her wig at Disneyland," or serious, such as "When Joey got baptized."

WEEK 5

Read and Record Books

"Nobody made a greater mistake than he who did nothing because he could do only a little."
—*Edmund Burke*

True story: Our next-door neighbor, Susan, was confined to a wheelchair with multiple sclerosis. She wanted badly to be of service, and we came up with this idea. She loved to read stories to children and then donate the book, tape, and book bag to our Head Start preschool. *Everyone* can be of service and make a difference!

Select one or more books suitable for preschool-aged children. The books can be new or gently used. You'll also need a tape recorder or digital recorder and a family member selected to be in charge of "technical support" and run the recorder. (Note: Most children today have CD players rather than tape recorders. Check with the school to which you will be donating the books before you begin your project.)

Decide how the book will be read. You could have each family member read one book or take turns with the pages. It might also be fun to have family members read the parts for various characters in the book. If you want, gather supplies to make sound effects.

Before you record, do at least one practice run. Make sure the sound is balanced well and that everyone can be heard.

Read the book into the recorder as practiced. Slowly and clearly read the title of the book and the author's and illustrator's names. Then read the book. Be excited and animated in your speaking. As you turn the pages, say, "Next page" or, "We're turning the page" so that the child who receives the book will know to turn the page at that point.

Play back the recording to make sure it sounds right. You may want to record several readings and pick the best one.

When you are finished, make a good copy of the tape or CD. Wrap the book and the CD together. If you want, put the package in a book bag. Many schools like this idea because the children can use the bag to carry home the book/recording they have checked out.

Have the entire family deliver the book and the recording to the location of your choice. We recommend donating it to your local Head Start program or a nearby preschool. Head Start locations can be found at http://www.acf.dhhs.gov/programs/hsb. ("Head Start and Early Head Start are comprehensive child development programs that serve children from birth to age five, pregnant women, and their families. They are child-focused programs and have the overall goal of increasing the school readiness of young children in low-income families.")

MODIFICATIONS

Young children: Have young children help choose the books you will record. Young children can also turn pages, make sound effects, and so on.

They can even do a "review" at the beginning and tell why they really like this book.

Teens: Have teens buy one of the books with their own money.

FAMILY DISCUSSION STARTERS

How do you get ready to go to school when you're young? (Talk about how some families don't have the education or money to provide this readiness.)

How did you learn to read?

Why is education important? (Talk about President Hinckley's encouragement to "Be Smart.")

How can education help end poverty?

FAMILY HOME EVENING IDEAS

Song: "Follow the Prophet," *Children's Songbook,* 110.

Story: Discuss how Mommy and Daddy went to school and what it was like. Have them talk about college or career training if it applies.

Article: Study President Gordon B. Hinckley's article, "A Prophet's Counsel and Prayer for Youth," *Ensign,* January 2001, 2–11.

Treat: Make chocolate cake mix cookies (combine 1 chocolate cake mix, 2 eggs, ⅓ cup oil. Drop batter into balls on a cookie sheet and bake at 375 degrees for 8 to 9 minutes). After cooling, add yellow frosting stripes and a "stinger" to make bumble bee cookies.

Activity: Take an "education" tour and visit local schools with your family. Have the children show you their classrooms and talk about their educational experiences. Visit Mom's and Dad's schools if they are nearby.

Extended: Choose a book to read aloud as a family. Read together each night until it is finished.

FireFighter Appreciation Day

"Asking why I incorporate community service into my teaching is a little like asking why I incorporate breathing into living."

—*Bob Hansman, Associate Professor, Washington University in St. Louis*

Contact your local firefighters' organization and ask how many firefighters are at your fire station and when it would be convenient for the family to come by.

Decide as a family how you want to show your appreciation to your firefighters. Ideas include:

- Making homemade treats, such as cookies or brownies
- Making a giant poster with candy bars that create a message like, "You may SNICKER when we come, but we think you're worth a HUNDRED GRAND!" Make sure your message is long enough so that each firefighter gets some candy.
- Making a giant thank you card or banner that the whole neighborhood signs
- Making each firefighter a cute pillowcase or pillow that says, "Thank you"
- Making gift bags with candy, a thank you note, and other treats for each firefighter

- Making decorations for a particular holiday to decorate the fire station. Make them simple and not obtrusive so they don't get in the way of their work.
- Making a recipe file of the family's favorite recipes—firemen cook for themselves and for each other and are always looking for fast and easy recipes!

On the day you are to come, call first to confirm your appointment. Remind the children that if the firemen get called, they have to leave fast! Park where you won't block their way.

If the fire crew has time, you can bring a family game and play with them or have them give you a tour. Make sure that each family member expresses his or her thanks for the great work the firemen do.

MODIFICATIONS

Young children: Try to schedule the family visit when the children can get a quick tour of the fire station and sit in the fire truck. Explain to them that they have to be flexible in case the firemen get called away. Make sure the firemen know you're bringing young children; they usually have freebies for little kids.

Teens: Have teens ask the firefighters about their scariest or weirdest run. Also talk to them about the preparation they had to go through to become firemen. Some fire stations will let teens go on a ride-along if it is arranged in advance.

FAMILY DISCUSSION STARTERS

What do our firemen do for us?

How would we feel if our house were burning and they came?

What do paramedics do?

What is the Burn Institute and what do they do to assist burn victims? (http://www.burninstitute.org)

What fire safety tips can we learn? (Talk about emergency exit routes; stop, drop, and roll techniques; and so on.)

FAMILY HOME EVENING IDEAS

Song: "The Wheels on the Fire Truck," sung to the tune of "The Wheels on the Bus." ("The wheels on the truck go round and round"; "the hose on the truck goes swish, swish, swish"; "the ladder on the truck goes up and up"; etc.)

Story: Discuss the events of September 11, 2001, and the rescue efforts of the firemen involved (many stories are available on the Internet).

Article: Study Richard M. Romney's article, "First to Aid," *New Era,* February 1999, 12–16.

Activity: Visit the fire station and play a game with the firefighters (a short one!).

As a family, practice having a fire drill. Have everyone go to his or her beds and have a parent set off the fire alarm. Arrange a place outside to meet as a family and discuss the importance of not leaving that place until someone else knows you're out safely. Practice checking the door, crawling out of the house, using two exits, doing the drill with your eyes closed, etc. Children can practice climbing out of their windows, using a chain ladder if they're on the second story. (The author has fond memories of practicing climbing out her bedroom window and down the rope to the ground, with her daddy timing the whole family on their safe exit!)

Heart Attack a Grandma

*"I promise you that if you'll use your gifts to serve someone else, you'll feel the
Lord's love for that person. You'll also feel his love for you."*

—*Elder Henry B. Eyring*

True story: My elderly mother called one day and said she'd had a heart
attack. . . . "What?!?" I yelled in shock. "And you didn't call!" She laughed
and told me her front yard was covered with hearts. She was delighted!

For this project, gather white, pink, and red construction paper. Have
the family cut out hearts—lots of hearts—large and small. Then use markers to write "love notes" all over the hearts. The notes might read, "We love
you!" "Have a wonderful year!" or "You're an incredible lady!" Add stickers and glitter if you'd like.

After the hearts are made, go to the home of a widow or single woman
who needs cheering up. Make sure you go when she's not home, or do it
quietly at night.

Decorate her front porch, windows, plants, trees—anything that is
standing still! Be careful not to attach tape to painted surfaces.

You can either doorbell ditch if you're doing this in the evening (be very
quiet!) or just let her discover the hearts on her own. It'll make her day!

MODIFICATIONS

Young children: Explain the importance of keeping a secret if you want to keep this one quiet.

Teens: No modifications needed.

FAMILY DISCUSSION STARTERS

Do you think it would be difficult to live alone?

How would you feel if someone gave you a "heart attack"?

How will it make this sister feel?

FAMILY HOME EVENING IDEAS

Song: "Love One Another," *Hymns,* no. 308.

Story: Discuss the story of Naomi in the book of Ruth.

Article: Study President Thomas S. Monson's article, "The Fatherless and the Widows: Beloved of God," *Ensign,* August 2003, 3–7.

Treat: Make a treat from a recipe handed down from your grandma.

Activity: Get out pictures of your grandmothers and talk about their lives. Then have the children role-play the stories and perform. Sing your grandmas' favorite songs and play their favorite games.

ASSeMble a HygieNe Kit

"We must not, in trying to think about how we can make a big difference, ignore the small daily differences we can make which, over time, add up to big differences that we often cannot foresee."

—*Marian Wright Edelman, founder, Children's Defense Fund*

True story: Our oldest son, Connor, was in Africa last summer and wrote: "The other day was a favorite of mine for the trip. Last fall I organized a service project in my ward to raise money for and put together hygiene kits to be sent to Zambia through Mothers Without Borders (the organization I'm over here with).

"We raised over $3,000 and put together 900 kits. Each kit had a hand towel, washrag, six toothbrushes, tube of toothpaste, and two bars of soap.

"I delivered the kits to the Mothers Without Borders warehouse, and that was that.

"So you can imagine my surprise when I was sitting in a village called Julius here in Zambia, helping out in the medical screening room by cleaning and dressing the wound of a young child, and I looked up to see one of the local staff membes handing out one of these hygiene kits.

"Full circle. It was such an honor to be able to see these kits being given away to those I had intended them for. I look forward to posting pictures here for all to see, and taking them to my fellow ward members so they can see those kits being given away to those who needed them most.

"It was a great day. . . ."

Read the story in the Family Home Evening Ideas section to help motivate family members, then decide together how many hygiene kits you want to assemble.

Gather the items listed here and assemble according to the directions that follow.

- 2 unbreakable combs (no sharp handles)
- 4 toothbrushes (packaged)
- 1 tube of toothpaste (6 to 8 ounces, no pumps)
- 2 bars of soap (approximately 4 to 5 ounces)
- 2 15x25-inch new hand towels (to sew your own towels, see directions below—do not use dish towels or wash cloths)

Items should be placed in heavy-duty gallon-sized plastic bags. Bags must be sealable; remove air before sealing.

To sew your own hand towels, use terrycloth cut in 15x25-inch rectangles. Serge or zigzag the edges to prevent fraying.

Completed items may be shipped or delivered in person to:

Latter-day Saint Humanitarian Center
1665 South Bennett Road
Salt Lake City, Utah 84104

Completed items may also be taken to the nearest bishops' storehouse or Deseret Industries. Seal boxes and mark them Latter-day Saint

Humanitarian Center–SLC. They will then be shipped to the humanitarian center. Locations of bishops' storehouses and Deseret Industries stores may be found by calling 801-240-5954.

Some Deseret Industries stores have a Humanitarian Service Room where volunteers may learn more about humanitarian service projects and have opportunities to serve. Locations of Humanitarian Service Rooms may be found by calling 801-240-5954 or online at http://www.provident living.org.

MODIFICATIONS

Young children: Let children do household chores or other small projects to earn money to buy items for the kits. Children can also help you pick out the items at the store. If you have very young children, be careful with the plastic bags.

Teens: Let teens buy the supplies with their own money. The story in the Family Home Evening Ideas section will help motivate them.

FAMILY DISCUSSION STARTERS

What items are in each hygiene kit?

What would you do if you didn't have those items to use every day in your life? (Talk about how crucial the items are to people after disasters hit.)

How would you feel if a disaster hit our area and you received one of these kits?

FAMILY HOME EVENING IDEAS

Song: "Today, While the Sun Shines," *Hymns,* no. 229.

Story: Discuss "Learning to Hope," a story by Mariama Kollon, as told to Riley M. Lorimer (*New Era,* November 2006, 10–12; you should edit as needed for younger children).

Talk: Study Bishop H. David Burton's talk, "Tender Hearts and Helping Hands," *Ensign,* May 2006, 8–11.

Treat: Make a treat from another country and talk about that country. (You can get treats in the ethnic foods section of your grocery store.)

Activities: Have the children try the following activities:

- brushing their teeth with no toothbrush
- combing their hair with no comb or brush
- washing their hands and faces and then running around to try to dry them without a towel

You could also have a hygiene-kit relay. Follow these directions (adjust the difficulty to suit different ages):

1. Divide into two teams if possible.

2. Place two plastic bags on a table at one end of the relay and two chairs—with supplies for a complete hygiene kit on each chair—at the other end of the relay course.

3. Start at the end with the plastic bag. Have the first player on each team run to the other end, pick up the toothbrush without using his or her hands or mouth, and run it back without dropping it. Each team must fill its own plastic bag with each item.

4. The next player has to run to a chair, pick up the toothpaste with his

or her feet, and crawl back (holding the toothpaste with his or her feet) without dropping it.

5. The next player has to run to a chair, grab the combs, put them on his or her body somewhere (perhaps in the hair), and run back.

6. The next player has to run to a chair, tie the towels around his or her body somewhere—using only one hand to tie—and run back.

7. The final player has to run to a chair, pick up the soap, and juggle it from hand to hand as he or she runs back.

If players drop any item, they must return it. The next player can then attempt to get the same item. The first team to fill its plastic bag wins.

WEEK 9

Bake Sale For the Hungry

"The bread in your cupboard belongs to the hungry man; the coat hanging unused in your closet belongs to the man who needs it; the shoes rotting in your closet belong to the man who has none; the money which you hoard in the bank belongs to the poor. You do wrong to everyone you could help, but fail to help."

—St. Basil the Great

Have the family first choose a charity to which they will donate the proceeds of the bake sale. Recommendation: Mothers Without Borders for use in one of their children's feeding programs. The purpose of Mothers Without Borders is "to address the needs of orphaned and abandoned children in a holistic manner." As they say on their Web site (https://motherswithoutborders.org/feeding.php): "We support efforts to provide safe shelter, food and clean water, education and access to caring adults. We want to assure that each child has someone who cares about them to teach them of their value. Thousands of orphaned and vulnerable children go hungry every day in Zambia, Zimbabwe and Ethiopia. Local communities struggle to provide for the growing number of orphans living in their midst. As a result, many children are forced to scavenge for food in trashcans and alleys, beg, or engage in prostitution. Mothers Without Borders supports local feeding programs designed to provide at least one meal a day to these children. $25 will feed a child for a month. Please help." Their address is Mothers Without Borders, 125 E. Main Street, Suite 402, American Fork, Utah 84003; and their telephone number is 801-796-5535.

Once you've selected your charity, set a fund-raising goal: how much money does your family want to earn to support efforts to feed children? Decide what items you will bake and where you will hold the sale. Locations could include a storefront (ask permission first), your home or yard, or another appropriate location. Make flyers to post around the neighborhood or send e-mail messages to publicize your sale. Send out a reminder e-mail the day before your sale.

Reserve the day before the sale for baking and packaging your goods.

Wrap all items for sale in plastic wrap and keep your hands clean during the sale. Have plenty of change on hand before the sale starts.

Next to your table, set up several large, full-color pictures from the charity's Web site as well as a stack of fact sheets with details about the charity you've selected. Place a jar on the table for contributions. You can also contact your charity ahead of time to get pamphlets or other literature that you can hand out to customers.

When people purchase items, ask them, "Do you want your change back or do you want to donate it to the cause?" Many people will let you keep the change. Before customers leave, say, "Thank you so much for supporting our bake sale to raise money for the hungry orphans. You can make additional donations here (point to the jar) if you'd like. Thanks!"

The more you explain your charitable cause, the more generous people will be.

When you've raised all the money, rejoice! Take the money to the bank, deposit it in your checking account, and then write out a check or get a cashier's check to the charity you've chosen. You might want to include a note describing your family's bake sale and sending your best wishes to the charity.

MODIFICATIONS

Young children: Young children will love to help bake and decorate. Just make sure they keep their hands washed! At the sale, make sure they have a specific task so they'll feel useful and won't get bored. They can be greeters or baggers or hand out charity literature.

Teens: Have teens research the charity and present a report to the family ahead of time. Teens are very motivated by causes like this and can extend invitations to their friends, seminary classes, or church group to help contribute. If they're good bakers, let them make something fancy.

FAMILY DISCUSSION STARTERS

What is it like to go hungry? (Talk about what it would be like to eat only once a day or once every three days.)

What would you do if you didn't have any food in the house?

What does Matthew 25:40 ask us to do? (Discuss its literal direction to feed the hungry.)

FAMILY HOME EVENING IDEAS

Song: "Because I Have Been Given Much," *Hymns,* no. 219.

Story: Elder F. Melvin Hammond, "You Can Make a Difference," *New Era,* March 1991, 44–48.

Talk: Study Bishop H. David Burton's talk, "'Go, and Do Thou Likewise,'" *Ensign,* May 1997, 75–77.

Treat: Make rice pudding and talk about how much of the world eats rice as its staple food.

Activity: Make the treats for your bake sale—let everyone participate.

Placemats For Seniors

"Love begins at home, and it is not how much we do . . . but how much love we put in that action."

—*Mother Teresa*

Use large (at least legal-sized), stiff paper, such as poster board cut to fit or construction paper. Have family members decorate one side of the paper. Ideas for decorating include a holiday theme; glued-on family photos; stickers or cutouts; or handwritten notes. Be creative!

When you are finished, laminate the placemats at a local school-supply store or copy center (if there is a Lakeshore Learning Center nearby, you can laminate the placemats there for less than 30 cents a linear foot). Or you can cover the placemats with clear contact paper.

Have the family deliver the placemats to a local nursing home or senior center. You can deliver treats to go along with the placemats if you wish, but be sure to check with the care center to see what restrictions apply.

MODIFICATIONS

Young children: No modifications needed.

Teens: Some teens may prefer to make designs on the computer and print out color copies to attach to the placemats. Let them get creative! They could also write poetry on the placemats.

FAMILY DISCUSSION STARTERS

Why is mealtime important? (Talk about what goes on during family meals.)

What are some of your favorite family meal memories and/or favorite meals?

FAMILY HOME EVENING IDEAS

Song: "There Is Sunshine in My Soul Today," *Hymns,* no. 227.

Story: Discuss the story of the feeding of the 5,000 in Matthew 14.

Article: Study Janene Wolsey Baadsgaard's article, "Mealtime, Family Time," *Ensign,* September 1998, 22–27.

Treat: Make s'mores over the stove. Using a fork, toast marshmallows very carefully over the stove burner—parents, supervise carefully! Place toasted marshmallow between squares of graham cracker with a piece of chocolate in between. Yum!

Activity: Have spaghetti for dinner. Spread a big, waterproof tablecloth or tarp on the floor. Use paper plates. Have the family sit on the floor to eat. Eat spaghetti with other utensils (not silverware!), such as tongs, spatulas, etc. Cover up first! Halfway through, change the rules and say that no one can feed himself—family members must feed the person across from them, using fun utensils. Showers may be needed afterward!

Collect Magazines and Books For a Shelter

"The greatest compassionate service each of us can give
may be in our own neighborhoods and communities."

—*Elder Glenn L. Pace*

Ahead of time, contact your local shelter for the homeless or for abused women (your city or county government can provide you the contact information). Ask if they will accept donations of magazines and books. If they will not, try another shelter.

Send out an e-mail and/or paper flyer notifying friends and neighbors that you are collecting magazines and books for a shelter. Give them plenty of lead time, so they can collect a large stack of magazines and books.

On collection day, go around the neighborhood and to friends and family to collect the magazines. It's helpful to give each person a half-sheet flyer that explains how they can continue to donate their books and magazines to the shelter you have chosen. Include the shelter's contact information for future reference.

When you are back home, go through all the magazines and books and remove any that are inappropriate or in bad condition. Box up the remaining books and magazines. Deliver them as a family to the shelter.

MODIFICATIONS

Young children: Have young children go through their own books and select some to donate. This will make it more personal for the little ones.

Teens: Encourage teens to ask their friends for donations as well. They might want to buy a magazine subscription for the shelter with their own money.

FAMILY DISCUSSION STARTERS

Where would you go if you didn't have a home or an extended family?

What different types of shelters exist in our community?

How else can we help the shelter?

FAMILY HOME EVENING IDEAS

Song: "Count Your Blessings," *Hymns,* no. 241.

Story: Discuss the story of the prodigal son in Luke 15.

Talk: Study Elder Robert D. Hales's talk, "'Some Have Compassion, Making a Difference,'" *Ensign,* May 1987, 75–77.

Treat: Make soup, with each family member contributing an item of their choice.

Activity: Set up a big tent in your yard (or family room if it's really cold). If you have no tent, make a big shelter inside with blankets and tables. Have the family spend the night together in their sleeping bags. Sing songs and tell stories together.

Neighborhood Potluck

"The best thing to give to your enemy is forgiveness; to an opponent, tolerance; to a friend, your heart; to your child, a good example; to a father, deference; to your mother, conduct that will make her proud of you; to yourself, respect; to all men, charity."

—*Francis Maitland Balfour, Scottish embryologist*

As a family, select a good night to hold a neighborhood potluck dinner. Make invitations to the potluck, telling your neighbors the time, place, and what to bring. Have fun with the invitations! Ideas: Fill a balloon with paper strips that give the details; find and print color pictures of the neighborhood from an aerial photo (go to Google Earth), and add the potluck details on the bottom of the page; have the little children color a picture of each neighbor's family and add details below; fly a homemade kite with the details on it or on the bows on the tail, etc. Be creative! Be sure to ask for RSVPs so you know how many are coming, and double-check your guest list the week before.

The day before, send your children around to remind all the neighbors. If you need neighbors to bring chairs or other items, remind them! Decorate your house for the day of the event. It's fun to pick a theme and decorate at least the front door. You can do a holiday theme, a carnival theme, a TV show theme, or whatever suits your neighborhood.

As guests arrive, greet them and make everybody feel welcome. You might want to plan a few get-to-know-you games if there are neighbors who don't know each other. Have a sign-in, if you'd like, to collect emergency contact information (including e-mails) to give to each neighbor afterward.

Make sure there are fun activities for the younger children. You may want to take some time for the grownups to discuss neighborhood issues, such as safety, traffic, emergencies, etc.

After the evening is over, do a follow-up thank you to the neighborhood. Even a cute poster on your lawn will do the trick. Enjoy getting to know your neighbors better!

MODIFICATIONS

Young children: Have young children help plan activities for their little friends, such as coloring, playing outdoor games, watching DVDs, etc.

Teens: Have teens set up a "cool" location for their friends to hang out. Be sure to have snacks for them as well!

FAMILY DISCUSSION STARTERS

Why are neighbors important?

What do you think makes a good neighbor?

What makes a good neighborhood?

What can you do to be a good neighbor?

How can we make a difference for good in our neighborhood?

FAMILY HOME EVENING IDEAS

Song: "Love at Home," *Hymns,* no. 294.

Story: Discuss the story of the good Samaritan in Luke 10.

Talk: Study President Gordon B. Hinckley's talk, "Closing Remarks," *Ensign,* May 2005, 102–3.

Treat: Make a triple batch of cookies or brownies and share with your neighbors!

Activity: Take a walk or bike ride as a family and tour your neighborhood, looking first for something that starts with an A, then a B, etc., throughout the neighborhood.

Military Messages

"Some people give time, some money, some their skills and connections, some literally give their life's blood. . . . But everyone has something to give."

—*Barbara Bush, former First Lady, United States of America*

Contact your stake president, bishop, or branch president to obtain the names of members of your stake, ward, or branch who are currently deployed with the U.S. military. These leaders will likely have addresses as well. If not, you can contact their family members to get the correct address.

Talk with your family about the men and women of the military and what they are doing. Discuss what a serviceman or woman would like to hear that would help them feel appreciated and encouraged. If appropriate, write some important words on a paper or board to help children know what to write.

Have each family member write a postcard or letter to the servicemen or women on your list.

Drop the postcards or letters in the mail.

MODIFICATIONS

Young children: Have young children color a picture for the service member. Parents can write a simple note at the bottom. Have the child tell you what to write.

Teens: Encourage teens to be positive and encouraging and to talk about things they like in their notes.

FAMILY DISCUSSION STARTERS

What are the names of the six U.S. military services? (Army, Navy, Marines, Air Force, Coast Guard, Reserve/Guard.)

What do members of each service do?

What do you think it would be like to be deployed or on other service that takes you away from your family for long stretches of time?

Why is the military important?

FAMILY HOME EVENING IDEAS

Song: "Onward, Christian Soldiers," *Hymns,* no. 246.

Story: Discuss the story of the 2,000 stripling warriors in Alma 53.

Talk: Study President Gordon B. Hinckley's talk, "War and Peace," *Ensign,* May 2003, 78–81.

Treat: Print out on your computer the insignia of the Army, Navy, Marines, Air Force, and Coast Guard. Decorate cookies with frosting to match the insignia and have the family guess which arm of the service each represents.

Activity: Play Capture the Flag in your yard with your family. Here's how: Divide into two teams. Team 1 has the front yard and Team 2 has the backyard, or split a field between the two. The teams are given a time period, perhaps five minutes, to hide their flag in their part of the yard or field. (*Optional:* During this same five minutes, the teams can send out spies to see where the flag is being hidden, as well as lookouts to catch the spies.)

When the flag is hidden, call out that you are ready. Then you simply try to get the other team's flag. If you get caught and tagged by an opponent on his or her territory, you have to go to "jail" and can only be freed by one of your teammates who grabs you before that teammate gets tagged.

The first team to capture their opponent's flag wins. Or, to make it a little more difficult, you have to get the flag and then return to your own side without getting tagged.

This game is totally different at night in the woods!

Extended: There are other ways you can serve military families or Church members: send e-mails to soldiers from one of many Web sites; donate money for gift certificates to a base commissary or BX (this might be extremely nice to do for families of deployed servicemen); use Operation Dear Abby to send electronic greeting cards; or buy a USO Care Package that will then be sent with Department of Defense approval to a service member.

Charity Garage Sale

"There is no greater calling than to serve your fellow men. There is no greater contribution than to help the weak. There is no greater satisfaction than to have done it well."

—*Walter Reuther, President, United Automobile Workers*

As a family, decide what charity you will support with this effort. Recommendation: American Red Cross. ("The American Red Cross, a humanitarian organization led by volunteers, guided by its Congressional Charter and the Fundamental Principles of the International Red Cross Movement, will provide relief to victims of disasters and help people prevent, prepare for, and respond to emergencies." See http://www. redcross.org.)

Choose a date and time for your garage sale and begin setting aside items to be sold at the sale. You can invite neighbors to contribute items and let them know what charity the proceeds will go to.

Depending on your area, you might want to advertise your garage sale in the newspaper or by distributing flyers. If you'd like, you can contact the charity ahead of time to get some literature to hand out during the sale. Make sure you have enough tables lined up to show off your sale items.

The day before your sale, assemble all your items and begin to price them. Don't price too high! Make a big poster to advertise that all proceeds are going to your charity. Create a box or jar with a picture of your charity and label it "Donations." You can make more than one such container if your sale is big.

Make large signs (use really big letters and a big arrow so that people can read your signs if they're driving fast) and post them on main streets near your sale to direct people to the correct location. Make sure you have enough change and a lock-box to hold the money; assign an adult or older teen to watch over the money. It's also helpful to have a pile of plastic bags you can use to bag shoppers' items after their purchases.

On the morning of the garage sale, put out additional posters in good locations to direct traffic. You can use eye-catching balloons. If you choose the Red Cross, you could use red balloons by your signs and then have a bunch of red balloons in front of your house.

Organize your items on tables and make sure prices are easily seen with stickers or papers. Greet each person that comes with a smile and tell them you're raising money for charity. If they're ready to leave, invite them to make a donation if they'd like. Always be friendly!

If you want, sell cold drinks and baked goods to raise even more money.

Once you're into your sale about two to three hours, begin to lower your prices to move as much merchandise as possible.

When you're finished, either return items that didn't sell or contact a local charity to pick up large items. Load the rest in your vehicle and donate them to Deseret Industries or your local thrift shop.

Meet as a family to count the money. This is the exciting part! Convert the cash to a check and send it to your charity with a note describing what you've done.

MODIFICATIONS

Young children: Assign younger children a specific task, such as supervising the sale of a "25 cents and under" table or bagging items for shoppers. Make sure you watch children carefully to keep them safe from the street.

Teens: Have more assertive teens call out to people in the street, handle money, etc.

FAMILY DISCUSSION STARTERS

What does the Red Cross do?

Why is it important to be prepared for disasters, donate blood, or perform other activities of the Red Cross?

FAMILY HOME EVENING IDEAS

Song: "Choose the Right," *Hymns,* no. 239.

Story: Discuss the story of Clara Barton, founder of the American Red Cross. Visit one of these sites for information about Clara Barton's life:

http://www.lkwdpl.org/wihohio/bart-cla.htm

http://en.wikipedia.org/wiki/Clara_Barton

http://www.nps.gov/archive/anti/clara.htm

Talk: Study President Gordon B. Hinckley's talk, "The Faith of the Pioneers," *Ensign,* July 1984, 3–6.

Treat: Make white cupcakes and use red licorice to make the red cross of the American Red Cross.

Activity: Do a disaster preparedness scavenger hunt. Have each family member roll a pair of dice—the person with the highest number runs to find the item called out from the list below:

- the family's first-aid kit
- the family's supply of food
- the family's 72-hour kit
- a flashlight
- a candle
- the front door, with their eyes closed the whole way!
- stored water
- a tent or tarp
- scriptures
- tools
- phone numbers for the extended family
- the family evacuation list
- a blanket
- batteries

Letters to Grandparents

"Charity is a work of the heart. It is not merely affection, but the highest and strongest kind of love. It is the pure love of Christ. If we love the Lord with all our heart, it becomes easier to love others. And as we do, we become more like Him."

—*"Clothed in Charity"*

True story: This service project can change a life! After my husband's grandmother passed away, Grandpa had a hard time being happy about carrying on. So we began to send him letters every week—postcards from travels, pictures that the children would write notes on, puzzles we'd make, and so on. It transformed his life. Every week he'd tell the rest of the family about the letters he'd received that week. He began to be excited again about getting up in the morning and running (slowly) to check his mail. We were so grateful that we could write to him and help him feel loved.

To do this project, make a list of all the addresses of the grandparents in your family. Assemble stationery, envelopes, cards, postcards, pens, markers, stickers, and photos. Make sure you have plenty of stamps.

Discuss as a family what you can talk about with your grandparents. Talk about news, stories, testimonies, and special experiences you've recently had.

Have each family member write letters to each grandparent. Make sure everyone gets one. You might want to include pictures that the children have colored, family photos, or other interesting items with the letters.

Have the children address the letters, and then have the whole family drive to the post office to mail them.

Make extra notes or postcards to be mailed in future days. It would be fun to send one every day for as long as they last.

MODIFICATIONS

Young children: Have young children color a picture, then dictate to you a message that you can write on the bottom of their pictures. Write it exactly the way they say it.

Teens: Have teens print out a page with a full-color picture on the top half of the paper. They can write a personalized note on the bottom half.

FAMILY DISCUSSION STARTERS

What do you know about your grandparents? (Share stories of their lives with the children.)

What kind of example have our grandparents set for us? (If your children's grandparents are members of the Church, talk about how they gained their testimonies, where they served their missions, and other spiritual experiences they may have had.)

What do you think it's like to grow older and become grandparents?

How can we be supportive and appreciative of our grandparents?

FAMILY HOME EVENING IDEAS

Song: "Families Can Be Together Forever," *Hymns,* no. 300.

Story: Discuss a faith-promoting story about your grandparents.

Talk: Study Elder Gene R. Cook's talk, "Home and Family: A Divine Eternal Pattern," *Ensign,* May 1984, 30–31.

Treat: Make a treat that is a favorite of one of the grandparents. If you can't think of any, make a birthday cake for all the grandparents and sing "Happy Birthday" in their honor!

Activity: If you live in the same area as a grandparent, ask him or her to take you on a tour of the area and share a favorite memory.

Toy Collection Bonanza

"Being unwanted, unloved, uncared for, forgotten by everybody,
I think that is a much greater hunger, a much greater poverty than the
person who has nothing to eat."

—*Mother Teresa*

Contact your local shelter for the homeless or for battered women and children and discuss with them the donation of toys. Be sure you are aware of any rules or limitations they have.

Collecting toys can be done in one or more ways. You can put out a notice to your friends and family requesting donations of any toys—new or gently used. Or you can collect toys at local garage sales or from neighbors. When you go to garage sales, you can tell them you're collecting for a shelter and they will often give you the toys or allow you to come back at the end and collect any toys that were not purchased. Finally, you can go through your own house in search of toys! Allow your children to contribute toys that are meaningful as well.

Gather all the toys and clean each toy carefully with antibacterial cleaning products. Some stuffed animals can be safely washed in the washing machine—use gentle cycle and put them in a pillowcase first. Check for any tears or holes first, or you'll end up with a washer full of stuffing!

Discard any toys that are not safe or are too worn-out. Repair any toys that can be repaired safely.

After the toys are in good shape, box them up carefully. If there are a lot of toys, it is helpful to sort them by age or category.

As a family, deliver the toys you have collected. (Keep in mind that sometimes battered women's shelters will not allow you to drop off donations directly at the shelter but will direct you to their office. This is for the safety and protection of the women and children. Please honor this and explain it to your children if necessary.)

MODIFICATIONS

Young children: Discuss why the children at the shelter need the toys and, if possible, take the children on a tour of the shelter.

Teens: Have teens think of "teen" things that can be donated, such as clothes, books for teens, CDs, and so forth. Your teens can collect items from friends as well.

FAMILY DISCUSSION STARTERS

What do you think it's like to live in a shelter and to have no home?

What do you think it's like for children whose families are having troubles and what it would be like to have no toys?

What does it mean to be a "steward"?

FAMILY HOME EVENING IDEAS

Song: "Fun to Do," *Children's Songbook,* 253.
Story: Discuss the story of *The Velveteen Rabbit.*

Article: Study President Thomas S. Monson's article, "The Spirit of Christmas," *New Era,* December 1974, 15–19.

Treat: Make snickerdoodles, letting the children roll the balls of dough in colored sugars before baking.

Activity: Play baseball with a twist. At first base, have a hula hoop that the runner has to keep using until he or she can run again. At second base, have two balls that the runner has to juggle. At third base have a jump rope. Use a Wiffle ball and bat and have fun!

Gardening For the Hungry

*"Community service is wherever there is a need,
and whatever you think that you can do."*

—Glenn Davis, student, Washington University in St. Louis

Identify where in your community there is a need for food—this may be at your local food bank, a senior center, a needy part of town, or a family you know that is struggling. (Also, missionaries always need veggies!) Talk to the organization you choose (or the family) and discuss what types of fruits and vegetables they could use.

Gather the family and discuss the need for fruits and vegetables. Then plot out a family garden that will not only provide for you but also have a designated area where you'll grow food for the hungry. If you do not have land, consider making a small planter-pot garden. Be sure you put rocks in the bottom of your pots before you plant so there is good drainage.

Divide up all the chores necessary to care for the garden. Make each chore suitable for each family member's age—but make sure every member of the family participates. If you need advice, invite someone who has experience with gardens to come and meet with your family to help.

Once the garden begins producing, have the family participate in delivering the produce throughout the harvesting season.

MODIFICATIONS

Young children: Give young children their own special watering can or gloves. Try to make it as fun as possible. Teach them carefully the difference between weeds and plants. Be patient.

Teens: Teens may struggle with this commitment. Just keep reinforcing how much joy the produce will bring. Have them be in charge of certain activities that they *do* like. Make sure they're part of the distribution; if they are, they will be more likely to respond to that feeling of making a difference.

FAMILY DISCUSSION STARTERS

What is it like to go hungry?

Why are the vitamins and minerals in fruits and vegetables important to our bodies?

What does the Word of Wisdom teach us about eating fruits and vegetables?

How do you think the recipient will feel when he/she receives fresh produce?

FAMILY HOME EVENING IDEAS

Song: "A Poor Wayfaring Man of Grief," *Hymns,* no. 29.

Story: Discuss the story in 4 Nephi of the Nephites after Christ visited them and how they cared for their poor and hungry.

Talk: Study Elder Joseph B. Wirthlin's talk, "The Law of the Fast," *Ensign,* May 2001, 73–75.

Treat: Make vegetable soup and have everybody in the family choose a vegetable from the garden (or, if you're just starting your garden, from the grocery store) to put into the soup. Make carrot or zucchini or pumpkin bread from your garden.

Activity: Have a work day in the garden to really get it in shape. Make it really fun—there should be a lot of water involved!

FLoWer FairieS

*"Make it a rule . . . never, if possible, to lie down at night without
being able to say, 'I have made one human being at least a little wiser, a
little happier or a little better this day.'"*

—*Charles Kingsley, novelist*

True story: Our Relief Society did this project one week for the senior
sisters in the ward. It was hilarious! We were all out planting in the dark
and trying not to giggle. The senior sisters were delighted the next morning
and tried to figure out who had been there. We were all quiet about our
secret! Those flowers cheered them for months!

Choose one or more families you want to surprise. It's especially fun to
surprise widows or single-parent families. Take your family on a drive
to "scope out" the families' homes.

Then go to your local store to purchase flowers in pots. Make sure the
flowers are healthy and not too overgrown or root-bound (look at the
bottom).

When it's time to plant, gather the family, some work gloves, and
shovels, and sneak over to your recipients' homes. Now, fairies often come
at night, so it's especially fun to do this in the dark. Take flashlights and be
really quiet so you don't get caught.

Plant the flowers in a suitable location by the family's front porch or walkway where they will give them cheer (and where you can make a quick getaway!). If it's difficult to find an appropriate spot (or if they live in apartments), you can plant pots beforehand and then drop by and door-bell ditch the flowerpots on the doorstep!

MODIFICATIONS

Young children: Young children will enjoy having their own shovels or helping you pick out flowers. Encourage them to be quiet if you're doing it as a surprise!

Teens: If they drive, have your teens drive the getaway car.

FAMILY DISCUSSION STARTERS

How was the earth created?

What are several ways we can beautify the earth?

FAMILY HOME EVENING IDEAS

Song: "For the Beauty of the Earth," *Hymns,* no. 92.

Story: Discuss the story of the Creation in Moses 2.

Talk: Study Elder Bruce R. McConkie's talk, "Christ and the Creation," *Ensign,* June 1982, 9–15.

Treat: Make a cake and use piped, colored frosting to create a garden scene.

Activity: Take some time to plant flowers in your own family's yard. Let the children design what flowers and colors you will use.

Help a Primary around the World

"Faith is the first factor in a life devoted to service. Without it, nothing is possible. With it, nothing is impossible."

—*Mary McLeod Bethune, educator*

Ahead of time, obtain contact information for a Primary president in another country or another state. You can ask missionaries in your ward, family members who live out of state, or other ward members for the name and address of a Primary president in another country or state. Write to the president and ask her what kind of support or items she could use for her ward's Primary. If you'll be mailing a package out of the country, ask for recommendations to make that process easier.

You can either order the items from the LDS Distribution Center (www.ldscatalog.com) or ask for donations from friends and family. Some fun things to purchase or make include:

- scriptures or copies of the Book of Mormon, in which members of your family have written their testimonies
- pictures of your local Primary and letters from the children in your Primary
- posters and pictures of Church topics
- pictures of Jesus for each child in their Primary

- a photo montage of "A Day in the Life of Our Family" with pictures and captions showing how your family lives
- books, videos, workbooks, coloring books related to the gospel

MODIFICATIONS

Young children: Have young children color pictures of gospel stories.
Teens: Have teens write their own testimonies.

FAMILY DISCUSSION STARTERS

How does Primary help children all over the world? (Talk about how the Church is the same throughout the world.)

What do/did you like best about Primary?

How has Primary affected your life?

FAMILY HOME EVENING IDEAS

Song: "Hello, Friends!" *Children's Songbook,* 254.

Story: Discuss the history of Primary. For a brief introduction to the history of Primary, go to www.lds.org/pa. Select the *Primary* link, click *Introduction to Primary,* then scroll to the bottom of the page and select *History of Primary.*

Talk: Study Elder David B. Haight's talk, "The Primary Enriches the Lives of Children," *Ensign,* May 1978, 22–24.

Treat: The Primary colors are red, yellow, and blue, so look for treats in those colors or make sugar cookies and frost them with these colors. Or you can make a treat from the country where your sponsored Primary lives.

Activity: If you help a Primary from another country, search the Internet for games that the children play in that country and try them! This can be adapted for a Primary in another state. Or you can gather information on what they do there and write up activities or famous things in that place and play charades. (For example: If it were in Michigan, you could do canoeing, fishing, skiing, and on and on.)

WEEK 20

Lemonade Stand For Love

"Let us open our hearts, let us reach down and lift up, let us open our purses, let us show a greater love for our fellowmen. The Lord has blessed us so abundantly. And the needs are so great."

—*President Gordon B. Hinckley*

Select a charity to support with the earnings from your lemonade stand. Recommendation: CARE. ("CARE is one of the world's leading humanitarian organizations fighting global poverty. Founded in 1945 to provide relief to survivors of World War II, CARE quickly became a trusted vehicle for the compassion and generosity of millions. Our reach and mission have greatly evolved and expanded since. Today, CARE helps poor families and communities in some 70 countries create lasting solutions to their most threatening problems. CARE's integrated projects include emergency relief, community rehabilitation and longer-term projects in areas such as education, health and small-business development. Each year, CARE helps tens of millions of people around the world affect real, positive changes in their lives." See http://www.care.org/about/index.asp. Or for general information you may call 1-800-422-7385 Monday–Friday 8:30 A.M. to 6:00 P.M.)

The most important consideration with lemonade stands is location, location, location. Have a family business meeting and have the family decide on a great location for the stand where there will be plenty of traffic but where it will be slow enough for customers to stop (busy streets don't work!).

Brainstorm with the family about how to run the stand. You may make the lemonade ahead of time and then bring it to your location or you can bring materials to make it there. The key is to make sure it's cold. Ice and coolers are crucial. You can also offer other treats for sale.

Make a sign to promote your stand. Write the word *Lemonade* in big, colorful, kid-like letters to attract business. (Mom and Dad need to take backstage on this one!) Have the children dress in bright shirts and put out extra signs with arrows to direct traffic if you'd like. Keep them big, bright, and simple.

Make a poster that describes the charity for which you are raising money (keep the poster simple, big, and colorful). When a driver stops, call out, "We're raising money for charity! Want to buy some lemonade?" Be friendly and be bold. Ask customers if they want their change back or if they want to donate it. When they're done, say, "Would you like to make a donation to the charity?" (You can name whichever you've chosen.)

Good supplies to have on hand:

- ice
- ice tongs
- coolers
- cups (6–8 oz. cups are a good size)
- napkins
- paper towels
- water (things get sticky)

- lots of change
- lockbox for money
- donation jar with big sign
- lemonade
- extra treats for sale

Remember to keep your hands clean!

When you're finished, count your money and send it with a letter to your charity.

MODIFICATIONS

Young children: Make sure young children are supervised when you're near the road. Children are great at holding signs, scooping ice, and so on.

Teens: Let teens control the money. You could make smoothies instead of lemonade because teens love to make smoothies.

FAMILY DISCUSSION STARTERS

What is poverty?

What can governments or individuals do to help end poverty? (Discuss how we can take an active part in influencing our governments to help fight poverty.)

What are some long-term solutions to the problem? (If your children are young, talk very simply about how we can help the poor.)

FAMILY HOME EVENING IDEAS

Song: "Because I Have Been Given Much," *Hymns,* no. 219.

Story: Discuss the story of Mother Teresa. (You can find it on the Internet at http://nobelprize.org/nobel_prizes/peace/laureates/1979/teresa-bio.html.)

Talk: Study President Marion G. Romney's talk, "The Celestial Nature of Self-Reliance," *Ensign,* June 1984, 2–6.

Treat: Make lemon bars and lemonade!

Activity: Take a tour around your community to look at all the types of businesses that exist. Talk about how your community works economically to provide for the residents.

Birthday Cards For Kids

"Service is an imperative for true followers of Jesus Christ."
—*Elder Dallin H. Oaks*

Gather materials to be used for making birthday cards—blank note cards, envelopes, colored paper, cardstock, stickers, markers, crayons, glue, scissors, and so on. Talk to the family about children who live in the foster care system in your community. Brainstorm ideas about what kinds of birthday cards these children would like.

Have a card-making night where you make many cards, for all age groups and genders, that say "Happy Birthday" or "We love you!" Have the entire family sign each card. Do not seal the cards in the envelopes; simply slip them in the envelopes without sealing so the foster care people can decide who is an appropriate recipient of the card. Have fun making tons of cards!

Deliver the cards to your local children's foster-care facility. (Call your county government if you're not familiar with the location or contact information.)

MODIFICATIONS

Young children: Let young children color and cut to their hearts' content!

Teens: Let teens design their own cards—ones that are suitable for other teens.

FAMILY DISCUSSION STARTERS

What is foster care? How would it feel to be a foster child?

How important are simple things, like saying "I love you!" to children in foster care?

FAMILY HOME EVENING IDEAS

Song: "I'll Walk with You," *Children's Songbook,* 140.

Story: Discuss favorite family birthday memories.

Talk: Study Elder Ben B. Banks's talk, "Take Time for Your Children," *Ensign,* November 1993, 28–30.

Treat: Make ice cream sundaes with all the children's favorite toppings—be creative!

Activity: Allow each child to pick an activity and day in which he or she can have a special "date" with just Mom and Dad. Find a sitter for the other kids (or have older kids watch younger kids), and spend some time one-on-one with each of your kids.

Writing to the Missionaries

"There must be no diminution in our effort to carry the gospel to the people of the earth. In the future even more of our young men must prepare themselves to go out in service to the Lord. Our Christian acts must precede them and accompany them wherever necessary."

—President Gordon B. Hinckley

Gather the addresses of missionaries serving from your family and/or ward. Also gather stationery, fun family pictures, stickers, envelopes, and stamps. Make sure you're familiar with postage for foreign countries if appropriate (you can find this on the Internet).

Have family members write letters to all the missionaries. Family members can share news of the family or the ward or area where you live. You may need to talk with the family for a while so that everyone can come up with things to write about.

Be sure to include pictures where you can. You can add favorite scriptures, Church materials, favorite talks, and so on, where feasible.

Help family members address the letters and put on the appropriate amount of postage before mailing.

MODIFICATIONS

Young children: Have young children color a picture; write a simple note at the bottom, dictated by the children.

Teens: Talk with your teens about what it would be like to be a missionary and ask them what they'd want to read in a letter.

FAMILY DISCUSSION STARTERS

Find on a map or globe the area where each of the missionaries is serving.

What do you think it's like to go on a mission?

What challenges do missionaries face? (If applicable, have family members discuss their own missions.)

FAMILY HOME EVENING IDEAS

Song: "I Hope They Call Me on a Mission," *Children's Songbook,* 169; or "Called to Serve," *Hymns,* no. 249.

Story: Discuss the story of a family member who served a mission. If such a story is not available, discuss a story of a person in Church history who served a mission, such as Parley P. Pratt or Heber C. Kimball.

Talk: Study Elder David A. Bednar's talk, "Becoming a Missionary," *Ensign,* November 2005, 44–47.

Treat: Make a treat from one of the countries where a missionary is serving (check the Internet for ideas); or, if the missionary is from your own family, make his or her favorite treat.

Activity: Do a missionary relay race or obstacle course. Family members can do any of the following activities as you design your game:

- knock on every door in the house
- iron a shirt
- shine some shoes
- carry a stack of church books
- look up five scriptures fast
- ride a bike around the yard
- say hello in five languages
- tie a tie
- put on a white shirt, button it up, put on a tie, pants, belt, and shoes—fast!

Baked Treats Doorbell Ditch

"Charity should begin at home, but should not stay there."
—*Phillips Brooks, Episcopal bishop*

As a family, decide whom you would like to surprise with a treat. Think about the elderly, families going through a difficult time, new neighbors, and so on. Decide what you are going to make and when you'll deliver it.

On baking day, make sure you have all the necessary ingredients. Also, have the paper products, plastic wrap, ribbon, etc., that you'll need.

Have fun baking your treats together. Be sure that every family member participates. Ideas include: brownies, pies, quick breads such as zucchini or carrot bread, sugar cookies, etc. You may want to keep it simple and make one type of treat; or do a combination of several treats, depending on your time and family.

Be sure to let the treats cool, then wrap them in a pretty fashion—you can add candies, bows, etc., to make the plate look attractive. You can add a note if you'd like, such as "We love you!" "Thinking of you," "Happy Monday," or a silly poem that a family member has written.

Prepare the family for the "doorbell ditch" phase of your operation. Each family has their own method of doorbell ditching, but the key is to get the treat on the doorway or porch and notify the recipient by either knocking on the door or ringing the doorbell and then running. Don't get caught! Some people use cell phones to call the person—but beware of caller ID!

MODIFICATIONS

Young children: Doorbell ditching is always challenging with young ones. You can live dangerously and bring them along or let them be "lookouts" in the getaway car.

Teens: Let teens do the delivering or drive the getaway car.

FAMILY DISCUSSION STARTERS

Why is it important to do some service anonymously?

How fun is it to receive a surprise or a service without knowing who has done it?

FAMILY HOME EVENING IDEAS

Song: "'Give,' Said the Little Stream," *Children's Songbook,* 236.

Story: Discuss Valerie Ipson's story, "Mysterious Visitors," *Friend,* October 2004, 4–6.

Articles: Study these two articles on the "Secret Service": Pat Graham, "Sharing Time: Join the Secret Service," *Friend,* February 1982, 34–35; and "Secret Service," *New Era,* February 2003, 27.

Treat: Make extra treats for the family to share after delivering.

Activity: Cut out a bunch of paper hearts and distribute them to family members. Throughout the week, encourage the family to do little acts of kindness secretly and to leave a heart at the scene. Place a basket in a central location where the hearts can be put after they're used and the receiver can write a quick thank you! At the end of the week, talk about all the kind acts that were performed and how the family felt both giving and receiving them.

Record a Senior's History

"Never forget that the purpose for which a man lives is the improvement of the man himself, so that he may go out of this world having, in his great sphere or his small one, done some little good for his fellow creatures and labored a little to diminish the sin and sorrow that are in the world."

—William E. Gladstone, former British Prime Minister

Choose a senior relative, ward member, or neighborhood friend to visit and interview. Have a member of the family contact the senior to see if this is something he or she is interested in doing. Set up an appointment.

Have the family meet beforehand to generate a list of questions. You'll want to ask your friend about his or her childhood, teen years, courtship, marriage, children, jobs, school, etc. Type the search term *oral history* on an Internet search engine to come up with ideas for questions. There is also excellent information available at the Church's Family History Web site http://www.familysearch.org. Be sure to put the questions in order of importance and explain to the children that some seniors can tire easily or be forgetful, which requires flexibility in how many questions you can ask.

Set up the recording aspects of your visit. You can use a digital recorder, tape recorder, or even your iPod (this may be a great assignment for your high-tech teens). Be sure to practice ahead of time so you're familiar with the equipment. Bring extra batteries or power cords or tapes.

On the day of the visit, call in the morning to remind your senior friend of the visit. When you go to visit the senior, be sure to ask about his or her day and share any news so that you all feel comfortable.

Take turns as family members asking the questions. Check your recording to make sure it is working. Try not to interrupt the person while he or she is talking. You can ask simple questions to get facts in place ("When was that?" "Where were you when that happened?"), but try not to interrupt. Be approving and encouraging and interested as you listen. You can also ask about details that intrigue you ("How much did a gallon of gas cost then?").

Don't stay too long, and be sure to offer water to drink and small breaks. When you're finished, thank the person and give him or her a hug! Make a copy of the recording for the individual and ask his or her permission before giving out copies to anyone else—including relatives. It would be lovely to arrange a follow-up visit.

At home, make copies of the recording as permitted and label them carefully with the name, date, and location of the interview. Have your family send a thank you note to the senior as well.

MODIFICATIONS

Young children: Let young children ask some simple questions ("What was your favorite toy?" "Did you eat ice cream?") and encourage them to be part of the process. If you're going to a senior care center, talk about what it's like beforehand so the child knows what to expect and will not be frightened or behave poorly. Have extra toys or activities in case the child grows restless.

Teens: Be sure to include questions that are relevant to teens ("Who was your first girlfriend?" "How did you meet Grandpa?" "What did you do for fun?" "What was your first car?"). Also be sure to ask questions about major world events that occurred during the senior's life (World War II, first man on the moon, etc.). You can let teens be in charge of the recording.

FAMILY DISCUSSION STARTERS

What do you think it would have been like to live at the time our senior friend grew up?

How did the world change during that time?

How did the church grow during that time?

What important world events are going on now that you might one day relate to your grandchildren?

FAMILY HOME EVENING IDEAS

Song: "Dare to Do Right," *Children's Songbook,* 158.

Story: Discuss one of the stories shared by the senior.

Talk: Study President Gordon B. Hinckley's talk about his life, "Seek Ye the Kingdom of God," *Ensign,* May 2006, 81–83.

Treat: Ask the senior what his or her favorite treat is and make it!

Activity: Play charades using things related by the senior (surfing in the ocean, teaching school, driving his or her first car, wringing out the wash, fighting in the war, riding a bike on his mission, etc.).

PLaNt a TTee

"Kneel down to pray. Step up to serve. Reach out to rescue. Each is a vital page of God's blueprint to make a house a home, and a home a heaven."

—*President Thomas S. Monson*

True story: Years ago our home ward wanted to remember my grand-mother who had passed away and had been dearly loved. The ward members purchased a beautiful tree that they planted in her memory next to the ward meetinghouse. We have enjoyed that beautiful tree for years, and it still stands in her memory.

Discuss as a family where you would like to plant a tree. You may choose a favorite park, a person's home, the church grounds, a school yard, etc. You may want to plant the tree in memory of someone who has passed away. After generating several ideas, contact the owners to see if planting a tree is permitted and if there are any guidelines (location, tree type, etc.) that need to be followed.

You may purchase the tree or ask a local plant nursery to donate one. Take shovels, gloves, a bag of enriched soil, and the tree(s).

Take turns digging the hole for the tree. (Be very careful before you dig to locate sprinkler lines, gas lines, etc.) It is important that you dig the hole large enough—a general rule is twice as deep as the pot holding the tree and twice as wide. Mix in the good soil with the dirt you have removed from the hole.

Carefully remove the tree from its pot or box. Gently loosen the roots at the bottom with your hand. Have the family hold the tree upright as you plant it in the hole and fill the area around it with the mixed soil. Make sure that the tree is not too low (water will puddle and harm the tree) or too high (roots will be exposed or will not get enough water). Firmly step on the soil around the tree so that it is somewhat compacted and will hold the tree up straight.

Water the tree deeply once planted. If the tree is thin or young, consider putting in a strong pole next to the tree and tying the tree gently to it to give it support. Use garden ties or cut-up pantyhose to gently tie the tree to the pole.

You can plant more than one tree, but make sure that you leave enough space between trees for each tree to reach its full growth. You can check with the plant nursery to determine what the appropriate spacing is.

If this is a memorial tree, put a marker at the base of the tree.

Be sure that arrangements have been made for follow-up care of the tree—either by the family or the owner.

MODIFICATIONS

Young children: Have young children bring small shovels to help dig the hole. You can also bring small flowers for them to help plant nearby.

Teens: Have teens study how to plant trees and become the "experts."

FAMILY DISCUSSION STARTERS

Why are trees important to our earth? (Discuss with older children the process of photosynthesis—plants making oxygen.)

How do things that are planted and grow over time compare to your lives?

Why is it important to take care of our earth?

FAMILY HOME EVENING IDEAS

Song: "In the Leafy Treetops," *Children's Songbook,* 240.

Story: Discuss the story of Johnny Appleseed or read Shel Silverstein's *The Giving Tree.*

Talk: Study President Gordon B. Hinckley's talk about his walnut tree, "To All the World in Testimony," *Ensign,* May 2000, 4–6.

Treat: Make caramel apples and then plant the apple seeds outside!

Activity: Go to a park with good climbing trees and enjoy! Or find a tree swing. You can also play "Ring around the Rosie" around the base of a tree.

VoLUNteer For a CoMMUNity EVeNt

"As we go forward, may we bless humanity with an outreach to all,
lifting those who are downtrodden and oppressed, feeding and clothing the
hungry and the needy, extending love and neighborliness to those about
us who may not be part of this Church. . . . We have done well.
We have much to be grateful for and much to be proud of.
But we can do better, so much better."

—*President Gordon B. Hinckley*

True story: When the Cedar Wildfires swept through our San Diego area community, an evacuation center was set up. Hundreds of people went to the center to volunteer to help. Many families said, "Please let us help. We've brought our children and want them to help and be a part of this experience." We had children in charge of caring for all the pets that had been evacuated, teenagers working security, grandparents comforting evacuated children, and so on. I was impressed that even though no one asked for volunteers, hundreds of families felt the desire to help and showed up. Our community was forever changed by that outpouring of love.

Contact several local community groups to ask what events are coming up that could use volunteers. You may consider contacting your city government; the chamber of commerce; the local school district or PTA; the American Red Cross; a Rotary, Kiwanis, or Lions Club; the Boy Scouts; or any other community group. Review all the activities that are coming up and the types of volunteer opportunities that are available.

Discuss as a family the event for which you'd like to volunteer. Make a couple of backup choices as well. Contact the appropriate organization and sign up as volunteers.

On the day of the event, show up early! Bring water, sunscreen, hats, pens, paper, or other supplies as needed. You can wear matching shirts if you'd like.

Enjoy volunteering. Be positive, helpful, and enthusiastic. Be sure to volunteer for areas where you see a need. Make sure that you are safe as well. Most of all, be kind and friendly to everyone you see.

When you are finished, go to the leaders of the event and thank them for letting you participate.

MODIFICATIONS

Young children: Tell the organizers of the event the ages of your children and be understanding if they request that you not include young ones. Sometimes one parent can volunteer with the older children and the other parent can participate in the activity with the younger children. Be flexible! If young children are participating, supervise them carefully and have extra toys or activities for them if they grow restless.

Teens: Let teens take a leadership role in selecting and participating in this event.

FAMILY DISCUSSION STARTERS

What organizations play vital roles in our community?

Why are volunteers important in making a difference in our community?

How can we give back to the community?

FAMILY HOME EVENING IDEAS

Song: "Kindness Begins with Me," *Children's Songbook,* 145.

Story: Discuss the story of a member of your community who has made a big difference. Discuss Captain Moroni in the Book of Mormon and how he changed his community.

Talk: Study Elder Hugh W. Pinnock's talk, "The Blessings of Being Unified," *Ensign,* May 1987, 62–64.

Treat: Support a local business—go to a local ice cream store or small restaurant to enjoy a treat that is popular in your area!

Activity: Take a tour of your local community. Have the children conduct the tour like official tour-guides. Be sure to visit any historic locations in town.

Rock Art Sale

"My plea is—if we want joy in our hearts, if we want the Spirit of the Lord in our lives, let us forget ourselves and reach out. Let us put in the background our own personal, selfish interests and reach out in service to others."

—*President Gordon B. Hinckley*

First, have the family choose a charity they would like to support with the proceeds of the rock sales. Recommendation: LDS Humanitarian Services (go to http://www.lds.org/humanitarianservices for more information).

As a family, gather medium to large rocks (from the size of your fist up to the size of a grapefruit). You can find them by a creek, in an empty field, or wherever rocks grow in your area! Wash, scrub, and thoroughly dry the rocks.

Gather acrylic or patio paints and brushes. You can also gather coloring books or drawing books for ideas. Have the family draw their designs (faces are fun!) on the rocks with a soft pencil or with chalk. (Make sure you lay the rock flat first to determine what sides of the rock are easily seen.) Spread out newspapers to cover the area, then start to paint. You can also just paint words, like *Love* or *Dream,* and then add a few designs, such as polkadots or swirling lines. You can use larger rocks to make "Welcome" stones. Allow the rocks to dry thoroughly.

When the rocks are dry, spray them with an acrylic spray (high gloss or satin). Be sure to spray outside or in a well-ventilated area. (Young children should not use the spray can.) Use several coats of spray, allowing the rocks to dry thoroughly in between each coat so the paint will not drip.

Make sure the rocks are thoroughly dry before holding your sale.

You can either sell the rocks around your neighborhood or advertise with e-mails and flyers and hold a full-fledged sale. As with other fund-raisers, make posters and flyers that tell everyone you are raising money for charity and will be donating the money.

Have fun selling your rocks! Don't sell them too cheaply. People will be happy to support your charity by buying your beautiful rock art!

It would be fun to send a picture of your family and all your painted rocks to the charity with your check. They would enjoy reading about your efforts to support their charity. Have fun!

MODIFICATIONS

Young children: Make sure young children wear painting clothes—acrylic paints don't wash out of clothes!

Teens: No modifications needed.

FAMILY DISCUSSION STARTERS

What does LDS Humanitarian Services do? (Go to their Web site and read their latest newsletter to find out.)

How can we support the Church's great humanitarian efforts?

FAMILY HOME EVENING IDEAS

Song: "Lord, I Would Follow Thee," *Hymns,* no. 220.

Talk: Study Bishop H. David Burton's talk, "Tender Hearts and Helping Hands," *Ensign,* May 2006, 8–11.

Treat: Make sugar cookies and frost them to match some of the patterns used on your rocks.

Activity: Play marbles!

Service Scavenger Hunt

*"Giving kids clothes and food is one thing but it's much more
important to teach them that other people besides themselves are important,
and that the best thing they can do with their lives is to use them
in the service of other people."*

—Dolores Huerta, President, Dolores Huerta Foundation

True story: One evening the Scouts showed up at our house and offered
to do a small act of service. I was shocked! We are a very active family and
usually don't need help. And yet here they were—helping even us! It meant
a lot to me. So of course I asked them to clean the toilets! They did a great
job—and I enjoyed their service as well.

Have the family make a long list of services they could perform for the
average family—things like cleaning a toilet, sweeping the kitchen floor,
loading the dishwasher. Make each item something that will take no more
than fifteen minutes. Type up and print out the list. The family then needs
to decide whether to do this activity strictly as a service for others or to use
it as a fund-raiser.

If you decide on a fund-raiser, select the charity you will support and
make a small poster with information on this charity. I recommend your
local PTA.

Have the family gather supplies they might need to perform the services, such as cleaning supplies, yard tools, garbage bags, gloves, etc.

You can warn the families you are going to approach ahead of time or just surprise them! If you're turning this into a fund-raiser, it's best to advertise the scavenger hunt in advance so people will be prepared to donate when you come to the door.

At each door, show the family the list and tell them you're on a Service Scavenger Hunt. Ask them what they'd like to have you do. (If they're hesitant, tell them you're great at yard work or cleaning toilets!) Have the whole family participate.

If this is a fund-raiser, explain ahead of time that you are raising money for a charity or organization and that tipping is greatly appreciated. Have a jar with a poster, which you leave by the door for them to read about your organization.

Leave them with a smile, hugs, and maybe a little candy or other simple treat. Do not stay to visit a long time. Your goal is to get as much service done as you can! (So tear Mom away and don't let her gab!)

MODIFICATIONS

Young children: Include on your list little chores that young children can do. Most little ones love to clean mirrors with glass spray. Just be sure to supervise.

Teens: Have teens be creative about how they can help. After the first house, they'll be hooked! (Just don't go to their friends' houses or they'll be mortified!)

FAMILY DISCUSSION STARTERS

How does it feel to serve people you know?

How can you be sensitive to the needs of others around you?

Why is it important to receive service graciously?

FAMILY HOME EVENING IDEAS

Song: "Put Your Shoulder to the Wheel," *Hymns,* no. 252.

Story: Discuss the story of Queen Esther's service to her people in the book of Esther.

Talk: Study Elder Henry D. Taylor's talk, "Am I My Brother's Keeper?" *Ensign,* July 1972, 74–76.

Treat: Make caramel popcorn and use it to build a model of your neighborhood on a cookie sheet.

Activity: Invite another family to join you on an activity—do something that tourists would do if they visited your community.

CPR/First-Aid Week

"How wonderful it is that nobody need wait a single moment before starting to improve the world."

—Anne Frank

Decide as a family whether you will take a CPR class (for those aged twelve and older) or whether you will have a family home evening on first aid. You can also decide to do both.

For family members who are taking the CPR class, contact your local fire department or Red Cross office to find out when classes are available. You can also get private instructors to come to your home to teach you.

For family members who are too young to take the class, have a family home evening on first aid. Talk about the following topics:

- What to do in an emergency (see activity below)
- How to dial 911 (for little ones, unplug the phone and practice)
- General overview on how to do CPR
- How to perform the Heimlich maneuver
- How to perform artificial respiration (breathing)
- How to control bleeding
- How to deal with poisoning
- How to stop, drop, and roll

You can use the Boy Scout Handbook or the Boy Scout First Aid Merit Badge Book (borrow one from your Scoutmaster) as resources. Make sure you do lots of hands-on practicing.

MODIFICATIONS

Young children: Choose only three items to talk about and keep them simple.

Teens: Make sure teens get CPR-trained.

FAMILY DISCUSSION STARTERS

How can being prepared reduce our fears in an emergency?

How can we use our knowledge about these things to help others in emergencies?

How can our family be prepared to help those in need? (Discuss how the family can be safe and prevent problems. Also discuss how often these topics should be reviewed by the family. Our family holds this home evening about twice a year—when daylight savings time changes. Go to *Provident Living* at http://www.lds.org and study emergency preparation. Many resources are listed there.)

FAMILY HOME EVENING IDEAS

Song: "Do As I'm Doing," *Children's Songbook,* 276.

Story: Discuss the story of the good Samaritan in Luke 10 (a spiritual first-aid story!).

Article: Study the principles of being prepared as outlined in Norman C.

Hill and Richard M. Romney, "Surviving the Storm," *New Era,* May 2006, 24–28.

Treat: Make or frost gingerbread man cookies. Have fun "rescuing" the gingerbread men!

Activity: Play the "What If?" game. Have a parent or older child ask, "What if . . . an earthquake (tornado, flood, or whatever fits your area) hit?" Then have the family come up with a plan on how to respond. "What if . . . the pan caught fire in the kitchen?" Discuss many examples.

Children respond well to this game because it helps them face what could happen and receive information on how to handle it.

Build a family first aid kit. A fishing tackle box works great! For more suggestions, go to http://www.lds.org; then click on *Provident Living,* and *Emergency Preparation Resources.*

FHE For Friends

"We entreat you to minister with your powerful influence for good in strengthening our families, our church, and our communities. . . . Those who follow Christ seek to follow his example. His suffering in behalf of our sins, shortcomings, sorrows and sicknesses should motivate us to similarly reach out in charity and compassion to those around us."

—*President Howard W. Hunter*

Meet as a family to discuss another family or acquaintance they would like to invite to family home evening. Choose a date for the guests to visit. Your family can then make a fun invitation to invite them to join you. You may want to take some treats, put a message in a balloon, make up a puzzle or code, or create some other clever invitation to deliver to your guests.

Be sure to call them the day before to remind them of your special night.

For your family home evening lesson, pick a topic that will be interesting to your guests. It's fun to have your whole family participate and include your guests as well. You can have them join you in a game or activity, share personal experiences, make a treat together, and so on.

It would be very special for your friends to hear your simple testimonies, so try to have a time set aside during your home evening to do that. They will feel the spirit of your home and your testimonies.

MODIFICATIONS

Young children: If young children are involved, have simple games, skits, and lots of fun songs.

Teens: Let teens be in charge of a portion of the family home evening experience.

FAMILY DISCUSSION STARTERS

How would your family's life and experiences be different without the gospel? (Share your testimonies with each other. Talk about your feelings for your guests and what it's like to learn about the gospel.)

FAMILY HOME EVENING IDEAS

Song: "Hello, Friends!" *Children's Songbook,* 254.

Story: Discuss the story of the first converts in your family.

Talk: Study Elder M. Russell Ballard's talk, "Creating a Gospel-Sharing Home," *Ensign,* May 2006, 84–87; and President Gordon B. Hinckley's talk, "Family Home Evening," *Ensign,* March 2003, 3–5.

Treat: Make a favorite family treat to share with your guests or make a treat that you can work on together, such as frosted cupcakes or sugar cookies.

Activity: Play a get-to-know-you game. Many ideas are available on the Internet. You can do a Bingo-type game and list things you need to find (someone who has brown eyes, someone who speaks French, etc.). Or you can do a charades-type game where individuals act out places their family has been on vacation. Or you can do a trivia game that you make up beforehand.

ASSeMble a NeWborN Kit

"We can do no great things, only small things with great love."

—*Mother Teresa*

Before you begin, look up the guidelines for newborn kits by going to http://www.providentliving.org and selecting *Service Opportunities* from the column at the right. Click *Make Humanitarian Kits* to see current guidelines.

For each newborn kit, you will need the following items:

- 1 receiving blanket (refer to guidelines on the Web site)
- 4 single-thickness, 25-inch cloth diapers (use 100-percent cotton birds-eye cloth)
- 4 diaper pins
- 1 pair booties
- 2 bars Ivory soap (regular size)
- 1 layette gown (newborn size—see Web site for sewing directions)

Go shopping as a family to purchase the supplies needed to assemble at least one kit. Let the children contribute to this project with their allowance or earned money.

The family can make a receiving blanket or layette gown if desired. This is a fun project for the family to do together. When the kit is finished, seal it in a heavy-duty two-gallon plastic bag and deliver it to your ward or stake humanitarian leader or mail directly to:

Latter-day Saint Humanitarian Center
1665 Bennett Road
Salt Lake City, UT 84104

MODIFICATIONS

Young children: Have young children pick out some of the items to be included.

Teens: No modifications needed. They'll enjoy this—even the guys like to participate!

FAMILY DISCUSSION STARTERS

What disadvantages do babies born in impoverished countries face?

How can parents cope with providing for their babies when they don't have much money?

What do you think a kit like this will mean to parents and a newborn baby in an impoverished country or emergency situation?

FAMILY HOME EVENING IDEAS

Song: "Oh, Hush Thee, My Baby," *Children's Songbook,* 48.

Story: Discuss the story told in Diane Hoffman, "In a Heartbeat," *New Era,* March 1993, 12–14.

Article: Study President Gordon B. Hinckley's article, "Behold Your Little Ones," *Ensign,* June 2001, 2–5.

Treat: Make a rectangular sheet cake—cut it in the shape of a baby bottle and frost.

Activity: Get out family members' baby books and other baby memorabilia. Spend an evening looking through the items and sharing funny stories of each child as a baby.

Sew a T-Shirt Dress

"I am only one; but still I am one. I cannot do everything, but still I can do something; I will not refuse to do the something I can do."

—*Edward Everett Hale*

True story: Several years ago, our local chapter of Mothers Without Borders made more than 250 T-shirt dresses to send to orphaned children in an African village in Zambia. The chapter later learned that when the dresses arrived, there were not enough to go around. To decide who should get new dresses, the village girls were lined up so that the holes in their old dresses could be counted. If a girl's dress had more than ten holes, she received a new dress. If there were fewer than ten holes, the girl had to keep her old dress. The chapter was heartsick that so many were not able to have new dresses, and they immediately made 350 more dresses to be sent over!

Purchase one or more T-shirts in girls' sizes. Make sure they are made of durable fabric (thin ones do not work as well). For each dress, purchase approximately one yard of fabric (depending on the size of the shirt) that coordinates nicely with the T-shirt. This fabric will become the skirt of the dress. It's best to use cotton or cotton blends.

Wash the fabric and T-shirt; then have the family measure and cut the coordinating fabric and assemble the dress as follows:

Make the skirt for the dress by following these directions:

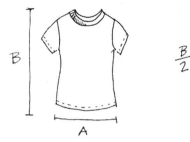

B

A

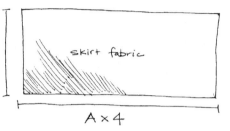

skirt fabric

$\frac{B}{2}$

$A \times 4$

1. Lay T-shirt flat on table and measure bottom of shirt (A). Then measure the length of the shirt (B).

2. Multiply shirt width (A) by 4. This will be the width of the skirt fabric. Divide shirt length (B) by 2. This will be the length of the skirt. Cut a piece of fabric to these dimensions.

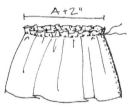

A + 2"

3. Fold fabric in half, right sides together, and sew the two short edges together. Then either serge or zigzag along seam edge. You'll end up with a large circle of fabric.

4. Run a gathering stitch along the top edge of the fabric circle about 1/2" from edge. Gather fabric until it equals the width of the T-shirt (A) + 2".

HEM

5. Turn skirt inside out and place T-shirt inside skirt. Pin gathered skirt edge to bottom edge of T-shirt, right sides together (hem edge of skirt facing up, gathered edge facing down). Sew gathered edge of skirt to bottom edge of T-shirt, stitching twice all around, and slightly stretching T-shirt to match gathered skirt edge (A + 2"). Serge or zigzag seam edge.

6. Flip gathered skirt down and lightly press the seam. Fold over the bottom edge 1/4-inch twice and stitch hem.

Contact Mothers Without Borders or another organization to make arrangements for donating your dress(es). Mothers Without Borders can be reached at http://www.motherswithoutborders.org or by calling 801-796-5535 or by writing to:

Mothers Without Borders
125 E. Main Street, Suite 402
American Fork, Utah 84003

MODIFICATIONS

Young children: Young children can help pick out fabric and T-shirts and match them up.

Teens: Teens should be able to make these from start to finish, particularly if you help them with the first one.

FAMILY DISCUSSION STARTERS

How would you feel if you had to wear dirty, torn, or worn-out clothing every day?

What would it feel like to get a brand-new dress for the first time?

How grateful are you for the clothes you have?

FAMILY HOME EVENING IDEAS

Song: "Count Your Blessings," *Hymns,* no. 241.

Story: If Mom has a story about her wedding dress, share it.

Talk: Study President Gordon B. Hinckley's talk, "'I Was an Hungred, and Ye Gave Me Meat,'" *Ensign,* May 2004, 58–61.

Treat: Make gingerbread or sugar cookies in the shape of girls and use icing in tubes to make dresses.

Activity: Have a family fashion show where family members show their favorite outfits or silliest outfits and modest outfits. Be sure to have a runway and music!

Pet Week

> *"The sweetness of true Christian service is often experienced in
> obscurity—in quiet rooms in homes and hospitals and places of
> confinement, in military barracks and refugee camps, and in other places
> far from public attention. Usually it is unheralded, but it reflects the
> standard set by the Savior for those who will 'inherit the kingdom
> prepared . . . from the foundation of the world.' (Matt. 25:34.)"*
>
> —*Elder Marion D. Hanks*

If you have a family pet, contact your local nursing home or senior center to arrange for your family to bring the pet to visit the residents. On the day of the visit, clean your pet thoroughly and take supplies to clean up after him if necessary. Walk your pet ahead of time outside to prevent accidents. Make sure you keep your pet calm as you visit the residents. Observe all guidelines of the facility you're visiting. You can even take in a fish bowl, hamster, or other small caged pet as permitted.

If you do not have a family pet, arrange for your family to visit your local humane society facility and volunteer. You can help wash animals, walk them, etc.

If that is not possible, offer to take the dog of a senior citizen or a family in your neighborhood to a local park or on a long walk.

MODIFICATIONS

Young children: Keep young children calm and supervised.

Teens: Have teens talk to the senior about pets he or she owned growing up.

FAMILY DISCUSSION STARTERS

How do animals bless our lives?

What animals are mentioned in the scriptures? (Discuss Adam naming the animals, Noah saving the animals, Balaam's donkey in Numbers 22—she talks!—and so on.)

FAMILY HOME EVENING IDEAS

Song: "The World Is So Big," *Children's Songbook,* 235.

Story: Discuss the story of a family pet or pets the parents had while growing up. Show pictures if possible. Discuss the story of Noah and the Ark for young children.

Article: Study David Collins's article, "Presidents and Their Pets," *Friend,* June 1976, 46–47.

Treat: Make a birthday cake in honor of your pet in the shape of a bone or other appropriate item.

Activity: Have a birthday party for your family pet. Be creative! Take your pet out for a walk or play at the park as appropriate.

Adopt-a-Park or -Trail Week

"Service to others is the rent you pay for your room here on earth."
—Muhammad Ali

True story: Every year I attend dinners held by our city to show appreciation to the volunteers in our community. I'm always impressed by one sweet family with three small children. They have adopted a trail that they hike and keep clean every week. The children are so proud of "their" trail and love to get their special volunteer pin every year. I'm proud of them!

Contact your local city, town, or county government (ask for the department in charge of parks and trails) and ask if your family can clean a park or trail. Set a time and date and obtain important details and guidelines about what you can and can't do.

On cleaning day, have the family wear suitable clothing and take work gloves, garbage bags, rakes, water bottles, and sunscreen. Clean the park or trail thoroughly. Be sure to do an "Itty-Bitty Pickup." This is where, after you've done an overall cleaning, you go back and pick up the little tiny bits of paper, plastic, glass, or metal that are lying around.

Be very safe—especially with glass. Also, be respectful of others using the trail or park. Remove all garbage (don't just fill up the park's garbage cans unless you are told to do so).

You can also make arrangements to permanently adopt the trail or park with the government department if you'd like. Just remember—this takes commitment!

MODIFICATIONS

Young children: Closely monitor younger children. Don't let them near glass, metal, or animal waste.

Teens: Let teens do the heavy-duty cleaning!

FAMILY DISCUSSION STARTERS

How do parks and trails benefit the community?

What is the history of our community?

How do you think our parks and trails were developed?

How are parks and trails paid for, used, and cared for?

FAMILY HOME EVENING IDEAS

Song: "You Can Make the Pathway Bright," *Hymns,* no. 228.

Story: Discuss the story of the Garden of Eden in Moses 2 and Genesis 1.

Article: Study Stanley B. Kimball's article, "The Mormon Pioneer Trail, 1846–47," *Ensign,* September 1979, 72–76.

Treat: Make a picnic lunch to eat.

Activity: Hike the trail you cleaned as a family or have a family picnic or play day at the park you cleaned.

Support Your Hospital Auxiliary

"I don't know what your destiny will be, but one thing I do know: the only ones among you who will be really happy are those who have sought and found how to serve."

—*Albert Schweitzer*

A hospital auxiliary is the organization associated with a hospital that helps in its fund-raising and volunteer efforts, as well as at the hospital gift shop. To contact your local hospital's volunteer auxiliary, call the hospital and ask for the phone number, or do a Google search with the hospital's name and the word *auxiliary* as search terms.

Once you reach the auxiliary, ask if you can make or purchase items to donate to its cause. I recommend making and decorating aprons or lap quilts to donate.

You can purchase ready-made aprons at a craft supply store. Using fabric paints or appliqués, decorate the aprons as a family. Let them dry thoroughly.

Lap quilts are easy to make as well. Purchase fleece. Decide what size you'd like the quilts to be, then add another 2 to 3 inches to that size on all sides. Mark and cut out the fabric. Make parallel cuts into the fabric at 1-inch intervals along all sides of the fabric. The cuts should be 2 to 3 inches deep. When you're finished, the quilt will have fringes all along the sides. Starting at a corner, take two strips and tie them together in a square knot. Do this with all the strips. Easy and fun!

Donate all the items you make by delivering them personally to the hospital. Have the auxiliary take you on a tour or show you what they do.

MODIFICATIONS

Young children: Supervise carefully.
Teens: No modifications needed.

FAMILY DISCUSSION STARTERS

What do you think it's like to be a patient in a hospital?
What do you think it's like to be a medical professional at a hospital?
How do volunteers help both the doctors and the patients at a hospital?

FAMILY HOME EVENING IDEAS

Song: "Healthy, Wealthy, and Wise," *Children's Songbook,* 280.
Story: Tell stories about the births of the babies in the family.
Article: Study the wonderful article on a priesthood quorum that serves the sacrament at a hospital, Matthew Baker, "Sacrament Service," *New Era,* October 2002, 20–23.
Treat: Make Jell-O—it's always a hospital favorite!
Activity: Take a tour of the hospital. (You may need to arrange this with the community relations department of the hospital, or you could ask your children's pediatrician to take you on a tour.)

Deseret Industries Drive

*"We often equate charity with visiting the sick, taking in casseroles
to those in need, or sharing our excess with those who are less fortunate.
But really, true charity is much, much more.
Real charity is not something you give away; it is something
that you acquire and make a part of yourself. And when the virtue of
charity becomes implanted in your heart, you are never the same again."*

— *Elder Marvin J. Ashton*

Contact Deseret Industries. (If you do not have a local DI, choose a donation location such as the Salvation Army or Goodwill Industries.) When you call, ask for a list of items not accepted for donation (usually these include mattresses, old records, etc.).

Put together a flyer and/or e-mail invitation for your neighborhood, family, friends, and other groups. Let them know that you are collecting items to donate to Deseret Industries.

Be sure to send several reminders; e-mails and phone calls work well.

Go through your house to gather any items you are not using. Be generous! Then take a van, truck, or carload of empty bags and boxes to your friends' and neighbors' houses to collect their items. You can either go from house to house or ask people to bring donations to your house or a central location. After all the items are collected, carefully go through the donations and throw away any garbage mistakenly included.

Deliver the donated items to your local Deseret Industries or other goodwill organization. This may take several trips!

MODIFICATIONS

Young children: Make sure you don't donate any of your children's items without their permission or you'll have some tears!

Teens: Put teens in charge of driving or loading.

FAMILY DISCUSSION STARTERS

What does Deseret Industries (or the Salvation Army, or other goodwill organization) do?

How can our unwanted or unused items help others?

FAMILY HOME EVENING IDEAS

Song: "I'll Walk with You," *Children's Songbook,* 140.

Story: Discuss the story of the widow's mite in Mark 12:41–44.

Talk: Study Elder Victor L. Brown's talk, "Blessing the One," *Ensign,* November 1979, 88–91.

Treat: Make a treat from food you got at the cannery.

Activity: Play Sardines as a family. Have one person hide while everyone else closes their eyes and counts. When the time is up, everyone splits up and tries to find the hider. When someone finds the hider, the game is not over! He or she quietly hides alongside the hider. Over time, several people will be hidden together, resembling a bunch of sardines.

The last person to find the hider loses that round. He or she is the next person to hide. Or you can reward the first person to find the hider by allowing that person to hide if he or she wants to.

Clean the Church

"What most people need to learn in life is how to love people and use things instead of using people and loving things."

—*Unknown*

True story: A family in our ward with two young girls regularly volunteers to clean the church. Their children do a great job and have a deep appreciation for the ward building. And the parents are teaching great lessons.

Contact a member of the bishopric to ask permission to clean your ward building.

Gather the family on cleaning day. Locate the cleaning supplies in the church (make sure you can open the building and the closet or room where the supplies are located). Assign various tasks to each family member: cleaning chalkboards, vacuuming, dusting, cleaning bathrooms, etc.

Remind the children that they are in the house of the Lord and that reverence is important. Do a thorough job—remember to straighten the rooms as well, removing items that need to go to the library or the lost and found.

Lock up carefully when you are finished.

MODIFICATIONS

Young children: Supervise young children and make sure they have something fun to do. They usually love spray bottles and paper towels!

Teens: No modifications needed.

FAMILY DISCUSSION STARTERS

How important is it to have a building to meet and worship in?

How should we treat and show respect for the building?

Where does the Church get the money needed to build our ward buildings and stake centers?

FAMILY HOME EVENING IDEAS

Song: "The Chapel Doors," *Children's Songbook,* 156.

Story: Discuss the story of the Peter Whitmer farm, which was the location of the first meeting of the Church. (Information can be found at http://www.josephsmith.net. Click on *Historic Sites* and then *New York.*)

Talk: Study President Gordon B. Hinckley's talk, "The Church Goes Forward," *Ensign,* May 2002, 4–7.

Treat: Make little churches out of graham crackers and frosting.

Activity: Bring bikes and riding toys and play in the church parking lot. (Teens might enjoy setting up a driving course, using chalk and cones. Drive carefully!)

WEEK 38

Paint-a-thon

"Never doubt that a small group of thoughtful, committed citizens can change the world. Indeed, it's the only thing that ever has."

—Margaret Mead, American cultural anthropologist

True story: Paint can do wonderful things! My favorite painting project was in Lusaka, Zambia, painting the Mothers Without Borders Children's Farm with a team of other volunteers. We painted the inside of their orphanage light blue and then painted the walls with flowers, stenciled sports balls, and a big African mural. We transformed the place! The children were amazed and delighted. A little paint goes a long way: Toward the end, we had only a small bucket of paint left and too much space to cover. It was absolutely miraculous to see how far that paint stretched. God works amazing miracles in very small things.

Before you begin your painting project, survey the area you'd like to bring to life. Painting options are varied. You might choose to paint a widow or widower's house, front door, or interior walls. Or you can contact a local volunteer organization to see what other options are available in your city. You might try the United Way or go online to www.volunteermatch.org. Type in your zip code for a list of volunteer projects available in your area. It's likely that a paint job will be somewhere on the list.

Once the project is chosen and a date is set, gather all of the needed supplies. (Don't forget gloves and hats or bandanas!) Bring paint, rollers, pans, brushes, edgers, cleaning supplies, stir sticks, plastic sheeting, edging tape, etc. Remember to dress in painting clothes.

Be very careful when doing the prep work. Tape off all windows and metal and cover any furniture, plants, etc., with plastic sheeting. Take care to do it right, and be sure you clean up very carefully as well.

Have fun during the process! If it's a big project, invite another family or two to participate.

MODIFICATIONS

Young children: Give young children a small area to paint or a specific task. Make sure they are very carefully supervised.

Teens: Teens love big paint rollers and extension handles. They'll go to town!

FAMILY DISCUSSION STARTERS

How did this project help beautify someone else's environment?

What are the emotional benefits of having a beautiful place to live?

Compare caring for our homes and communities with the care that goes into constructing our temples. What are some of the comparisons?

FAMILY HOME EVENING IDEAS

Song: "Head, Shoulders, Knees, and Toes" (which are hopefully not covered in paint!), *Children's Songbook,* 275.

Story: Discuss the story of the building of the temple closest to where you live and talk about its unique features.

Article: Study "President Hinckley and the Nauvoo Temple," *Ensign,* July 2002, 24–25.

Treat: Make sugar cookies and frost with a paintbrush. (Thin the frosting with milk to make this easier.)

Activity: Make a craft that needs to be painted. Use the crafts as a decoration or for gifts.

If you're brave, let the children paint their closet doors or part of your house. (In our children's bathroom, the walls are covered with glossy, brightly colored handprints of all the children. They love to see how they've grown over the years.)

WeLcoMe Baby Day

*"When was the last time you unselfishly reached out to help another
in need? Every time we cheer another's heart, every time we ease another's
burden, every time we lift a weary hand, we show our gratitude to that God
to whom we owe all that we have and all that we are."*

—*Elder Joseph B. Wirthlin*

Identify a family with a brand-new baby in your ward, neighborhood, or family. Contact the family and offer to bring dinner one night.

Have your family work together to prepare a lovely dinner. Make a good dessert as well. Make sure you make something the family will enjoy (it's okay to ask what they like) and that you make enough. Take the meal in disposable containers so the mother does not have to worry about returning dishes.

Also prepare a small toy, blanket, book, or other gift to be given to the new baby from your family. You can make it or have the children help you select something from the store. If there is only one other child in the family, such as a toddler, it might be wise to bring that child a small gift as well (a ball or bubbles are good ideas).

As a family, deliver the dinner and the small gift. Have a nice visit with the family and admire the baby and congratulate them. A short visit is pleasant.

MODIFICATIONS

Young children: Make sure young children are healthy and have clean hands before touching the new baby. It's also wise to ask the new mother for permission before anyone holds or touches the baby.

Teens: If the new mother permits, make sure your teens have a chance to hold the baby.

FAMILY DISCUSSION STARTERS

What does it feel like to have a new baby join a family?

Why is it important to support families at this time in their life?

How does having a baby change the family's experience and routine? (Discuss the joy each of your family members brought to the family when they were new babies.)

FAMILY HOME EVENING IDEAS

Song: "A Happy Family," *Children's Songbook,* 198.

Story: Discuss one of the stories about babies in the scriptures (Moses, Samuel, John the Baptist, or Jesus, for example).

Talk: Study Elder Russell M. Nelson's talk, "Reverence for Life," *Ensign,* May 1985, 11–13.

Treat: Get squeezable cheese and the family's favorite crackers. Use the cheese to "write" each family member's initials on the crackers. (Or you could use cookies with spray whipped cream.)

Activity: Have a baby relay race, using dolls as the babies. Each family member takes a turn doing the following:

- diapering the baby
- feeding the baby
- burping the baby
- walking the baby
- singing to the baby
- dressing the baby
- rocking the baby

Food For the Homeless

"Succor the weak, lift up the hands which hang down,
and strengthen the feeble knees."

—*Doctrine and Covenants 81:5*

True story: My sister Andrea made two turkeys and fixings for Thanksgiving. Then her family, with other friends, took the extra food to the freeway underpass in downtown Salt Lake City. They served a Thanksgiving meal to the homeless who gathered there. Her children always came home more appreciative of what they had and more loving to others.

Contact a local homeless shelter or soup kitchen. Ask what the age requirements are for helping. If your children are all old enough, volunteer to come one day to help prepare and serve a meal. Ask for any guidelines so that you are properly prepared.

Before you go, discuss with your family what to expect and how to behave. Dress simply that day. Bring happy smiles and friendly spirits. Make it a fun and positive experience for the children.

If you have young children, you can do a food drive for your local shelter or food bank instead (or do it in addition to serving at the soup kitchen). Type your state's name and the words *food bank* in an Internet search engine to get contact information. Go through your own cupboards and collect food you'd like to donate. Have the children think of what food they'd like to receive (not just get rid of).

You can then collect food donations from your neighborhood, extended family, friends, or co-workers. Be sure to collect canned or dried food and to avoid food stored in glass jars or bottles.

Box the food carefully and deliver it as a family to the shelter or food bank. While you are there, it would be nice to take a quick tour so your family can be familiar with your local service. You may want to do this several times a year.

MODIFICATIONS

Young children: Let young children collect food from the cupboard and pantry.

Teens: No modifications needed.

FAMILY DISCUSSION STARTERS

What do you think it's like to live with the fear of not having enough to eat?

How blessed are we to always have food?

Why is it important to value this blessing?

FAMILY HOME EVENING IDEAS

Song: "A Song of Thanks," *Children's Songbook,* 20.

Story: Discuss the story of Elijah and the widow of Zarephath and her son in 1 Kings 17. Share Colleen M. Pate's story, "Giving Our Best," *Friend,* September 2006, 29.

Talk: Study Elder William W. Parmley's talk, "'Come, Follow Me,'" *Ensign,* November 2003, 93–94.

Treat: Make a soup or stew with all the leftovers in your refrigerator. Be creative!

Activity: Have a cooking party where the family looks through the cookbook and chooses a completely new recipe to try.

WEEK 41

Librarian Appreciation Day

"If I can stop one heart from breaking, I shall not live in vain;
If I can ease one life the aching, Or cool one pain, Or help one fainting
robin Unto his nest again, I shall not live in vain."

—*Emily Dickinson*

Contact your local library and ask how many librarians work there.

To show appreciation to the librarians, have the family make "thank you" pins. Assemble supplies:

- small safety pins or other fastening pins
- colorful cardstock
- duct tape
- stickers
- glue (craft glue or hot glue sticks)
- glitter
- bright markers

Make pins by cutting the cardstock into a square, rectangle, or other shape no larger than 2x3 inches. Decorate the pin any way you'd like, with the words, "Thank you" or "Best Librarian!" or "We love our librarian" or whatever you'd like. Let the family be creative.

Affix the safety pin to the back using a strip of duct tape or a dab of hot glue. Try the pin several times to make sure it is secure and works properly.

You can also bake a plate of goodies or make cards.

Take your thank you items to the library as a family and make a presentation to the librarians (you must whisper, of course) and tell them how much you appreciate them. Pin on their pins and give them big hugs. They'll be so surprised!

MODIFICATIONS

Young children: No modifications needed.

Teens: No modifications needed.

FAMILY DISCUSSION STARTERS

Why are libraries important in our community?

What do librarians and volunteers do to help a library to run?

How are books and education important in our family?

FAMILY HOME EVENING IDEAS

Song: "Book of Mormon Stories," *Children's Songbook,* 118.

Story: Discuss the story of the writing of the Book of Mormon and keeping of the records.

Article: Study President Gordon B. Hinckley's challenge in "The Book of Mormon: Read All about It," *New Era,* September 2003, 4–7.

Treat: Make brownies and use tube frosting to write book titles on the squares.

Activity: Take a tour of the library and try out all the things available there. Have the entire family get library cards.

WEEK 42

Art Gallery Fund-raiser

*"Savior, may I learn to love thee, Walk the path that thou hast shown,
Pause to help and lift another, Finding strength beyond my own."*

—Susan Evans McCloud, LDS author

As a family, choose an organization to support with the proceeds of your sale. Recommendation: the Boy Scouts, Girl Scouts, or a Boys and Girls Club.

Begin to gather artwork for your sale. Invite children from all over—your family, your neighborhood, your ward, or other groups—to either come to your home to make artwork or to deliver it to you. You can have the children do paintings, chalk drawings, pencil drawings, sculptures, or any other kind of art. Be sure all work is identified carefully with the child's name and age.

As a family, review the artwork you have gathered. Select the pieces that you will frame. Purchase (or make) inexpensive frames and frame as much of the art as possible.

Advertise your art sale with flyers and e-mails that announce the date, place, and time of your "gallery opening." Invite all the families of the children who have submitted artwork and ask them to invite their extended families and friends. You can even invite your local newspaper to come cover the event.

On "opening day," set up your yard, garage, or home like an art gallery. Borrow (and label with the names of those you borrowed from) lots of easels. Use beautiful fabrics to cover tables. Display sculptures and framed works on the tables and easels. Make it as fancy as you can.

It's fun to have a mixture of art throughout. Pay attention to the lighting in the "gallery" and arrange art so it is presented to its best advantage. Have classical music playing in the background. If desired, serve water and appetizers to guests as they browse.

At the entrance, have your children (dressed in their finery) welcome the guests. Have them explain to the guests that they are raising money for the Boy Scouts (or whatever organization you have chosen to support). Have a small handout (you can get them from the organization for free) that describes the purpose of the organization.

You can either mark the artwork with small price stickers or you can just leave it up to the guests to set a fair price. Have labeled donation jars set tastefully throughout the area. At the end, set up a small table where your older children can accept "payment" or donations for the artwork purchased. Graciously thank guests as they leave.

You can have talented children also play the piano or another musical instrument or do small performances if you would like. If you have some really nice art pieces, you can have an auction at a certain point in your event to get higher prices for those pieces.

Make this event elegant and delightful! Recognize the children as "artists." They'll *love* it! Take pictures and send them with your donation, explaining about your wonderfully successful art gallery sale.

MODIFICATIONS

Young children: Explain in advance that you are selling their artwork so they don't get upset when someone takes it home!

Teens: Have teens submit their work. Get their talented friends to contribute as well and you'll get some real quality art. For the day of the event, have your teens borrow a tux or a fancy dress from friends so they can look really outstanding.

FAMILY DISCUSSION STARTERS

What contribution does art make to a community?

What type of art do you like?

What role does art play in a civilization? (Discuss the importance of bringing beauty and refinement to the world.)

FAMILY HOME EVENING IDEAS

Song: "All Things Bright and Beautiful," *Children's Songbook,* 231.

Story: Discuss the story of your favorite artist. Do a search on the Internet to find information about the artist.

Talk: Study President Boyd K. Packer's talk, "The Arts and the Spirit of the Lord," *Ensign,* August 1976, 60–65.

Treat: Make Rice Krispies treats or caramel popcorn and let the family make sculptures while the mixture's still warm.

Activity: Go to your local art gallery or museum to view the art in your area.

RaKe/SHoVeL/SWeep tHe NeigHborHood WeeK

"In our homes, those small and simple things—our daily acts of charity—proclaim our conviction, 'Here am I; send me.'"

—Anne C. Pingree, former counselor, Relief Society General Presidency

Make a flyer to notify your neighborhood that you will be performing this service. (Depending on the time of year, you can rake leaves, shovel snow, or sweep!)

On the work day, dress appropriately. Knock on your neighbor's door (so they're not startled to look out and see a work crew) and say hello. (Ignore the protests of, "You don't need to do this!" Just agree and say, "We know we don't have to—we *want* to!" and get to work!)

Clean your neighbor's walkway and driveway. Then move on to the next house. See how many you can serve, and have fun!

MODIFICATIONS

Young children: Make sure young children have a broom to help.

Teens: Let them use the power blowers.

FAMILY DISCUSSION STARTERS

How do you feel when you help keep your home and neighborhood beautiful?

How can neighbors support one another in this effort?

FAMILY HOME EVENING IDEAS

Song: "I Have Work Enough to Do," *Hymns,* no. 224.

Story: Discuss the story of buying your home and moving in. As parents, talk about the neighborhood in which you grew up.

Talk: Study President Thomas S. Monson's talk, "Never Alone," *Ensign,* May 1991, 59–62.

Treat: Visit your favorite ice cream parlor.

Activity: Have a fix-up day at your own home, so it looks nice for the neighborhood.

CHarity CataLog DoNatioN

"May we be generous with our time and liberal in our contributions for the care of those who suffer. May we commit to the principles of Good Samaritanism and be ever mindful of the need to 'go, and do thou likewise.'"

—*Bishop H. David Burton*

This project is a wonderful opportunity for your family to buy a very unique gift for a family or village in a third-world country.

Have a family meeting and review the charity catalog of your choice. Recommendation: the *Heifer International Gift Catalog.* Heifer International provides animals of all kinds to families and villages so that they can use the animals to provide for themselves. For example, you can buy a goat, which villagers can milk and breed, and then have the offspring to sell. You can buy a flock of chickens, which villagers can raise for eggs and meat and chicks to sell.

Heifer International's mission, simply stated, is "to end hunger." As they state on their Web site: "Heifer envisions . . . A world of communities living together in peace and equitably sharing the resources of a healthy planet.

"Heifer's mission is . . . To work with communities to end hunger and poverty and to care for the earth.

"Heifer's strategy is . . . To 'pass on the gift.' As people share their animals' offspring with others—along with their knowledge, resources, and skills—an expanding network of hope, dignity, and self-reliance is created that reaches around the globe."

To learn more and to get a catalog, visit Heifer International's Web site at http://www.heifer.org.

After browsing the catalog, decide as a family what animal you would like to purchase and donate.

There are a number of ways you can provide the money for this gift: you can have the children save money they earn all month or all year long; you can have the children give up part or all of their Christmas or birthday presents (i.e., the money that would have been spent on them); or you can have them do a fund-raiser. You can also have your children collect money throughout your neighborhood. If you do the latter, have the children take around pictures of the animal you will purchase and literature about Heifer International. It makes the experience much more meaningful if every family member contributes and sacrifices. After you purchase the animal, print out a picture of it and have the family name it! You can also print out a map showing where your animal is going.

MODIFICATIONS

Young children: No modifications needed. Just let them work and earn money (even if it's only a small amount) so they feel that they are part of the experience.

Teens: No modifications needed. You can let them buy a flock of chickens with their own $20.

FAMILY DISCUSSION STARTERS

Why is it important to help people sustain themselves? (This term is referred to as "sustainable development" on the Internet. You can look it up and discuss it together.)

FAMILY HOME EVENING IDEAS

Song: "Who's on the Lord's Side?" *Hymns,* 260.

Story: Discuss the story of the Jaredites preparing the barges in the book of Ether and talk about how the Lord helped the brother of Jared, but also wanted him to help himself and come up with solutions to his problem.

Article: Study President Marion G. Romney's article on temporal salvation, "Principles of Temporal Salvation," *Ensign,* April 1981, 3–7.

Treat: Make a giant cookie in the shape of the animal you have purchased.

Activity: Make an obstacle course in your backyard (some fun ideas are available on the Internet). Use what you have on hand—car tires, a rope tied in a tree, a kiddie pool, anything that can be made into an obstacle. Have family members run the course once and then try to beat their own times or divide into two teams. Encourage them to do their best at overcoming obstacles in their path.

CHarity BirtHday Party

"The world today speaks a great deal about love, and it is sought for by
many. But the pure love of Christ differs greatly from what the world thinks
of love. Charity never seeks selfish gratification. The pure love of Christ seeks
only the eternal growth and joy of others."

—*President Ezra Taft Benson*

This can be done for a parent or a child. When the selected individual's birthday approaches, have the family discuss turning the birthday party into a charity party. Have the family member pick his or her favorite charity. (If you need help picking a charity, try looking at www.usafreedom corps.com for ideas.)

When you send out birthday party invitations, include a note or half-sheet flyer indicating that this is a *charity* birthday party. Describe the charity you have chosen and list the type of donations needed. (For example, you could pick one that takes care of babies and request layettes, receiving blankets, diapers, onesies, etc.) Be very clear about what types of donations you're interested in and also tell them they can donate cash.

It could be fun to use the charity as a theme for the party. For example, let's say it's Mom's birthday and you're having a party to donate to an organization that takes care of abandoned babies. You could have the treats, decorations, and games all centered on babies—like a baby shower! Or, if it's Brother's birthday and he wants to donate to the African Wildlife Federation, you can use wild animals as the theme—make it fun!

MODIFICATIONS

Young children: Young children may not understand why they have to "give up" their birthdays, so don't start with them.

Teens: This would make an awesome teen party! They love parties—and they often are very charity minded.

FAMILY DISCUSSION STARTERS

How does the charity we have chosen accomplish their mission?
What else could we do to help the charity?

FAMILY HOME EVENING IDEAS

Song: "You've Had a Birthday," *Children's Songbook,* 285.

Story: Discuss the history of the charity you chose to support for this project.

Article: Study a wonderful birthday story in Kristen Winmill Southwick's "Birthday Temple Trip," *New Era,* February 2003, 28–31.

Treat: Make treats that match your theme. Get creative!

Activity: Match up games with your theme as well. There are tons of party games on the Internet.

FLag WeeK

*"Ask not what your country can do for you—
ask what you can do for your country."*

—*John F. Kennedy*

For Memorial Day or Veteran's Day (or a comparable holiday in your country), purchase or make small flags. Identify all the active duty military personnel and veterans you know. On that special day, or earlier in the week, take a flag to them and express your appreciation for their service.

If you want, you can expand this project and post small flags in all the yards in your neighborhood on Flag Day or another holiday.

You can also make small flag pins with beads and safety pins and give them out as thank yous.

MODIFICATIONS

Young children: No modifications needed.
Teens: No modifications needed.

FAMILY DISCUSSION STARTERS

What kind of service have veterans provided our country? (Discuss the wars that have been fought and the freedoms that the military protects in keeping your country safe. Discuss the story of a veteran from your family or a hero from your country's past.)

FAMILY HOME EVENING IDEAS

Song: "The Star-Spangled Banner," *Hymns,* no. 340.

Story: Study the story of Captain Moroni in the Book of Mormon.

Article: Study Elder L. Tom Perry's comments on the American Bicentennial in "God's Hand in the Founding of America," *New Era,* July 1976, 45–50.

Treat: Make a flag cake. Make a white sheet cake and frost with white frosting. For a U.S. flag, use cut-up strawberries and blueberries to make the stars and stripes.

Activity: Go to a local military cemetery and read the markers. If you don't have one, go to your local VFW (Veterans of Foreign Wars) chapter or to a historical marker for veterans in your community.

Make a Difference Day

"You must be the change you wish to see in the world."
—*Mahatma Gandhi*

Have a family meeting to decide how your family would like to participate in the national Make a Difference Day. "Make a Difference Day is the most encompassing national day of helping others—a celebration of neighbors helping neighbors. Everyone can participate. Created by *USA Weekend* magazine, Make a Difference Day is an annual event that takes place on the fourth Saturday of every October. Millions have participated. In 2005, 3 million people cared enough about their communities to volunteer on that day, accomplishing thousands of projects in hundreds of towns. Your project can be as large or as small as you wish! Look around your community and see what needs to be done" (for more information, see their Website at http://www.usaweekend.com/diffday).

Be sure to have your planning meeting well in advance of October so you can be prepared to participate on that special day!

MODIFICATIONS

Young children: If you pick a project suited for young children, no modifications should be necessary.

Teens: Let teens help research ideas on the Internet.

FAMILY DISCUSSION STARTERS

What impact does volunteerism have on the community, the country, and the world?

How do you feel about volunteering?

How can one person make a difference? (Talk about people you know who are making a difference.)

FAMILY HOME EVENING IDEAS

Song: "Scatter Sunshine," *Hymns,* 230.

Story: Discuss the story of King Benjamin in the Book of Mormon and the influence he had on his community.

Article: Study Geri Christensen's article, "The Name Game," *New Era,* March 1991, 49–50.

Treat: It's October, so make your favorite fall treat! You can make pumpkin bread, toasted pumpkin seeds, or pumpkin cookies, among other things.

Activity: Do a fall activity that matches your climate.

Trick-or-Treat For UNICEF

"One mentor, one person can change a life forever.
And I urge you to be that one person."

—*George W. Bush*

Have a family meeting at the end of September and discuss having the family participate in "Trick-or-Treat for UNICEF." "UNICEF—the United Nations Children's Fund—is working in 156 countries to provide health care, clean water, nutrition and education to children and their families. And by Trick-or-Treating for UNICEF, you can help kids around the world too!"

What you do is order trick-or-treat boxes from UNICEF, and then take them along when you go trick-or-treating. Contact the United States Fund for UNICEF (see their Website at: http://www.unicefusa.org/site/ pp.asp?c=hkIXLdMRJtE&b=1706865) to obtain the collection boxes. Have the entire family participate!

MODIFICATIONS

Young children: Allow young children to both get candy and ask for UNICEF donations.

Teens: Have teens collect from friends as well.

FAMILY DISCUSSION STARTERS

What is the United Nations and how does it work?

What does UNICEF do to help children around the world?

FAMILY HOME EVENING IDEAS

Song: "Children All Over the World," *Children's Songbook,* 16.

Story: Discuss the story of Jesus blessing the children in 3 Nephi.

Talk: Study Elder Henry B. Eyring's talk, "That We May Be One," *Ensign,* May 1998, 66–68.

Treat: Make Halloween treats! A favorite of ours is cake mix cookies. Take any cake mix, add 2 eggs and ⅓ cup oil (no water). Mix thoroughly. Drop small balls onto an ungreased cookie sheet and bake at 375 degrees for 9 minutes. You can use any kind of cake mix, but a white cake mix with ½-inch slices of a Snickers candy bar placed on top of the dough ball before baking is heavenly.

Activity: Have the whole family trick-or-treat through the neighborhood together. Take flashlights! Make Mom and Dad dress up!

DoNate HaLLoWeeN CaNdy

"That best portion of a good man's life,
His little, nameless, unremembered acts of kindness and of love."

—*William Wordsworth*

A number of organizations might welcome your leftover Halloween candy. These include homeless shelters, battered women shelters, foster care facilities, nursing homes, or even Meals on Wheels. Choose a group and contact them to see if they are interested in receiving the candy.

Invite families in your neighborhood to join you in your project by dropping off any candy they're not keeping.

Sort through the candy and get rid of any unwrapped or opened candy. Also remove any candy that is in Halloween wrapping. Take the remaining candy and divide it between plastic bags. Tie each bag with a pretty ribbon (curling ribbon works well).

Deliver the candy as a family.

MODIFICATIONS

Young children: Don't let them eat it all!
Teens: Ditto!

FAMILY DISCUSSION STARTERS

How do we feel when we give up something we want?

How can this help us be better people?

FAMILY HOME EVENING IDEAS

Song: "It's Autumntime," *Children's Songbook,* 246.

Story: Discuss a time when a family member had to make a sacrifice to do something better or to help someone.

Article: Study President N. Eldon Tanner's article, "Sacrifice," *Ensign,* June 1981, 2–6.

Treat: You're probably tired of so much sugar, so make a salty treat! You can make soft pretzels and turn them into interesting shapes, like fall leaves. Salt the pretzels, dip in mustard if you'd like, and enjoy! A good recipe can be found from Robbie Price at http://robbiehaf.com/Recipes/A/69.htm.

Activity: Play Flashlight Hide and Seek outside in the crisp fall air! Here's how:

"It" holds the flashlight (turned off) and counts to fifty. All the kids hide while "It" counts. "It" looks for the other children with the flashlight turned off. When he finds a child, he shines the flashlight on him. That child now takes the flashlight and goes to find the other hiders. This can go on for a while without "It" having to recount and other players having to rehide.

Christmas Jar

"The reason charity never fails and the reason charity is greater
than even the most significant acts of goodness he cited is that charity,
'the pure love of Christ' (Moro. 7:47), is not an act but a condition or state
of being. Charity is attained through a succession of acts that result in
a conversion. Charity is something one becomes."

—*Elder Dallin H. Oaks*

Get a big jar and decorate it as desired. Put the jar in a prominent location in the home. Throughout the year or month, have the family throw in all their loose change and any extra money they want to contribute.

Just before Christmas, meet as a family to decide who will receive the money in the jar. It's best to pray together about this and ponder it together. If possible, make the donation a secret.

MODIFICATIONS

Young children: Encourage young children to do little jobs throughout the year and contribute some of their money.

Teens: Make sure you discuss the jar throughout the year so that they remember.

FAMILY DISCUSSION STARTERS

What impact could our donation make on someone? (Discuss examples of family members who have been helped by others—especially anonymously.) You might enjoy reading the book, *Christmas Jars* (or listening to the CD version) by Jason Wright about a family that has this tradition in their home. (*Christmas Jars* is published by Deseret Book, 2006.)

FAMILY HOME EVENING IDEAS

Song: "The First Noel," *Hymns,* no. 213.

Story: Discuss Wilma M. Rich's story, "Our Pickle-Jar Christmas," *Ensign,* December 1993, 15–18.

Article: Study President Thomas S. Monson's article "The Fatherless and the Widows: Beloved of God," *Ensign,* August 2003, 3–7.

Treat: Make a giant cookie in the shape of a Christmas tree and have the whole family help decorate it.

Activity: Go on a neighborhood (or ward) Christmas Service Sniper activity. Make up a list of things you can do for neighbors (outside only) that may include shoveling snow, putting a candy cane on a neighbor's door, washing a window, chalk-drawing a "hello" message on a driveway, singing carols, making a snowman, etc. Write down your list and number it (list 6 to 12 items and number them from 2 to 12). Take along a pair of dice and the supplies you'll need. Go to each house, roll the dice, and perform the service with the corresponding number.

Adopt-a-Family/Sub-For-Santa

"Jesus said love one another. He didn't say love the whole world."

—*Mother Teresa*

Contact an organization in your community that has an Adopt-a-Family or Sub-for-Santa program. (The local PTA, church, county government, or shelter are all good places to start.) Most programs of this sort begin in October or November. Prayerfully pick out a family to adopt.

Have a family meeting to discuss your budget, your money source (remember the value of having children participate in working for and saving some of the money), what the family's needs are, and timing and delivery issues. Some organizations will let you talk directly to the family to assess what their needs are.

As a family, shop or make the gifts. Don't forget necessities. Popular things are new socks, new toothbrushes, T-shirts, gift cards from grocery stores, and other necessary items. Include some fun items—even for the grown-ups. You can include also a "baking kit," made of flour, sugar, brownie mixes, chocolate chips, and so on.

As you prepare, think about what the family would want—not just what you want to give them. It's fun to include some Christmas items as well—treats, decorations, silly socks, or whatever you'd like.

If you personally deliver your gifts to the family (some organizations handle it this way and others do not), please be very sensitive. This is a time to express great love and support—not to show off how wonderful you are. The emphasis is on *them*—and they want love, not pity. Big hugs are always in order.

MODIFICATIONS

Young children: Have the children help pick out toys. Help them think about what that child would want. They can also color pictures or make things to give to the family.

Teens: No modifications needed.

FAMILY DISCUSSION STARTERS

How are all families different?

How are all families alike?

What can our family do to be supportive and Christlike to other families?

FAMILY HOME EVENING IDEAS

Song: "Oh, Come, All Ye Faithful," *Hymns,* no. 202.

Story: Discuss the Book of Mormon events leading up to Christ's birth. Talk about what it was like for families who were members of the Church through that time.

Article: Study President James E. Faust's article, "A Christmas with No Presents," *Ensign,* December 2001, 3–7.

Treat: Make Rice Krispies treats. Add green food coloring to the mixture before shaping into small wreaths and decorate with red candies for berries.

Activity: Choose a new activity to make a family tradition. It may be going sledding, skiing, to the beach to play football, or any other activity. Add traditional elements—have everybody wear red, drink cocoa and eat donuts, or whatever you want to make it into a tradition.

TWeLve-Day Nativity

*"It's not enough to say we believe and that we love Him; we must
be found possessed with His kind of love for others at that last day. It is not
necessary for us to lay down our life for others as He did, but like the Savior,
we should bless the lives of others by giving of what our life is made up
of—our time, our talents, our means, and ourselves."*

—*Elder Robert J. Whetten*

Buy or make a nativity set with twelve pieces: Mary, Joseph, donkey,
stable with manger (crèche), oxen, shepherd, sheep, 3 wise men, angel, baby
Jesus.

Choose a family to surprise. Each day, deliver one piece of the set with
a note attached. The note can be printed out in a cute font or handwritten. Decorate the notes as a family.

1. **Mary:** Think of Mary. Elder Bruce R. McConkie said, "We cannot
but think that the Father would choose the greatest female spirit to be the
mother of his Son, even as he chose the male spirit like unto him to be
the Savior" (*The Mortal Messiah,* 1:327). Nephi saw Mary in a vision and
described her as "A virgin, most beautiful and fair above all other virgins"
(1 Nephi 11:15). She was also described as "a precious and chosen vessel"
(Alma 7:10), "blessed . . . among women" (Luke 1:28).

Mary was just a young, teen-aged woman when the angel Gabriel appeared to her. "She was troubled" (Luke 1:29). How frightened and confused she must have been! Nevertheless, she listened to the angel as he told her that she would be the earthly mother of the Savior. She accepted her calling even though she did not completely understand what it meant. "Behold the handmaid of the Lord; be it unto me according to thy word" (Luke 1:38). Later, Mary rejoiced: "My soul doth magnify the Lord, and my spirit hath rejoiced in God my Saviour. . . . For he that is mighty hath done to me great things; and holy is his name" (Luke 1:46–47, 49). When Mary chose to do the will of God, peace filled her heart.

On this day, think about Mary and her love for her son, Jesus. Do we love Him?

2. Joseph: Ponder Joseph's life and role. He was a "just man" (Matthew 1:19). The Spirit must have taught Joseph throughout his life and guided him to become a man worthy of raising the Son of God on earth. He must have been an honorable, faithful man. And he loved Mary. They both followed the promptings that led them to each other. As Joseph learned that Mary was expecting a baby, he was understandably upset. What should he do? Should he chastise her publicly—that would be customary. Or should he just quietly break off their engagement?

As he pondered these things, the angel of the Lord appeared to him in a dream and explained to him that Mary had conceived "of the Holy Ghost" (Matthew 1:20). This beautiful young girl to whom he was engaged would be the mother of the Savior of the world. He should not be afraid to marry her, because she was indeed still a virgin, worthy of his love. Joseph listened, heeded the angel's counsel, and "took unto him his wife" (Matthew 1:24). He would act as earthly father to Jesus. When Joseph believed and submitted, he was at rest.

Think of the responsibility that Joseph bore to God's son. Do we keep our promises to Him?

3. The donkey: According to tradition, the donkey had the solemn task of carrying the mother of the Christ Child to Bethlehem, where the prophets had foretold that He would be born. He was a simple yet sturdy animal that would carry the mother of the Son of God. Jesus would later ride a donkey shortly before his crucifixion. Such a humble animal!

Here was the donkey, not knowing what a significant role he was performing in the unfolding story of the birth of the Savior. He was just doing his job. He had carried people before, and he would carry people afterward. But for these few days, his job would be vitally important. He would bring relief to sweet Mary, the chosen mother.

How many times do we show our willingness to just do the job—not worrying about reward or prestige? Are we willing to do the work of the Son? Are we willing to bear one another's burdens?

4. The stable: Ponder what it was like to be in Bethlehem at this time. It was a very, very busy time with extended families gathering in the Judean town from all over the region. The streets were thronged with people and animals and their burdens. It was noisy and chaotic.

The inn was bulging with customers, and the innkeeper and his wife likely struggled to feed and serve them all. Then yet another knock came at the door. There stood a young man with his very pregnant wife. We don't know exactly what happened next or how Joseph and his young wife were led to a stable in Bethlehem. We know only that there was no room in the inn.

It's likely, though, that the humble stable provided a quiet and calm respite from the bustle of the crowd. And it is in this same quiet way that we hear the still small voice and feel our Savior's love. Take the time to be still.

5. The oxen: The oxen stood quietly in their stalls, their warm bodies and breath keeping the stable warm. Who knows what they saw that night? They stood as silent witnesses to the birth of the babe and watched as Mary wrapped him in swaddling clothes. All of creation stopped in silent awe as the Son of God came into the world.

We are all witnesses of his love. We can speak of this truth—that he lives! Do we share our testimonies and stand as witnesses of this truth?

6. The shepherds: Luke records, "And there were in the same country shepherds abiding in the field, keeping watch over their flock by night.

"And, lo, the angel of the Lord came upon them, and the glory of the Lord shone round about them: and they were sore afraid.

"And the angel said unto them, Fear not: for, behold, I bring you good tidings of great joy, which shall be to all people.

"For unto you is born this day in the city of David a Saviour, which is Christ the Lord.

"And this shall be a sign unto you; ye shall find the babe wrapped in swaddling clothes, lying in a manger.

"And suddenly there was with the angel a multitude of the heavenly host praising God, and saying,

"Glory to God in the highest, and on earth peace, good will toward men.

"And it came to pass, as the angels were gone away from them into heaven, the shepherds said one to another, Let us now go even unto Bethlehem, and see this thing which is come to pass, which the Lord hath made known unto us.

"And they came with haste, and found Mary, and Joseph, and the babe lying in a manger.

"And when they had seen it, they made known abroad the saying which was told them concerning this child.

"And all they that heard it wondered at those things which were told them by the shepherds" (Luke 2:8–18).

The shepherds believed all that they had been told. And they immediately acted on what they had learned from the angel of the Lord. We too can receive direction from the Spirit. And then we can immediately act on what we're told. When we do, we will be blessed.

7. **The lamb:** It's likely that the shepherds brought with them the smallest lambs so they were not left in the cold. The lambs were so soft and white. Here they knelt, before the Lamb of God—he who was pure and sent from above to cleanse us all.

As we ponder the birth of our Savior, let us repent and give up our sins and the pull of the world. Let us make ourselves pure with his forgiveness.

8. **The first wise man:** In the East were the wise men, or Magi. According to the LDS Bible Dictionary, "Their identification is not made known in the scriptures, but it is certain that they were righteous men sent on an errand to witness the presence of the Son of God on the earth. Their spiritual capacity is evident: They were able to see the star when others could not; they knew its meaning, and brought gifts to the young child; and they were warned of God in a dream to return to their home by a safe route. Their knowledge was precise and accurate. It seems likely that they were representatives of a branch of the Lord's people somewhere from east of Palestine, who had come, led by the Spirit, to behold the Son of God, and who returned to their people to bear witness that the King Immanuel

had indeed been born in the flesh. We are not told how many wise men there were, but tradition usually speaks of three, because of the three gifts of gold, myrrh, and frankincense. If they were serving in the capacity of witnesses, there would of necessity have been two or three" (s.v. Magi).

They asked King Herod, "Where is the child that is born, the Messiah of the Jews?" Herod asked that they return after finding the child.

On they went to perform their mission—to witness the birth of the Savior of the world and to provide gifts for his family.

The Spirit of the Lord will lead each of us throughout our lives if we will listen. At this time, ponder what our particular missions are. Listen to the Spirit's promptings as we follow our paths in life.

9. The second wise man: The wise men followed the star, the new star that had risen in the evening sky. They followed the light until it shone directly upon where the mother and child lived. They visited the young family and presented their gifts of gold, frankincense, and myrrh. Together, the three types of gifts represent three roles of Jesus the Messiah. When the Magi presented gold, they were honoring Jesus with the very best that they possessed, and they were also recognizing that Jesus was King. Frankincense is highly fragrant when burned, and was, therefore, used in worship, where it was burned as a pleasant offering to God. It represents Christ's divinity. And the bitter myrrh was brought as a gift to acknowledge the human suffering that Jesus partook of when he came into our world. They brought him incense as their God, gold as their king, and myrrh recognizing his human body that was subject to suffering and death.

By these gifts, the Father inspired the Magi to then provide the means necessary for a long and expensive journey into Egypt, and to sustain

Joseph, Mary, and Jesus in a foreign land where they would stay for a considerable time.

How will God use our gifts to help build his kingdom? Do we offer those gifts freely? Ponder what gifts, strengths, and abilities we have that we can share with others.

10. The third wise man: The wise men had witnessed the reality of the Christ. It was time for them to return and bear witness to their people. Herod had requested that they report their discovery to him. However, the wise men were righteous men and heeded God's warning in a dream that they should not return to Herod. After they had found the child and witnessed that he lived and worshiped him and presented their gifts, Matthew records that they "departed into their own country another way" (Matthew 2:12).

We must resist temptation and the lure of worldly power as we go throughout our lives. We must heed the promptings that we receive and fearlessly pursue them. What are we afraid of? How can we have faith to do what we are prompted to do? Let us ponder on these things.

11. Angel: The angel brought good tidings of great joy. His job was to announce the arrival of the Savior—to Mary, to Joseph, and then to the shepherds. Then he was joined by a heavenly choir singing praises to the Lord.

Gather your family and sing "Joy to the World" or "Hark, the Herald Angels Sing."

Music is an important part of celebrating the birth of the Savior. Spend time this day singing carols out loud and feeling the spirit of the music.

12. Baby Jesus: The Savior came to the world, and he has come to us.

On this day, spend a moment to ponder our testimonies of him. As one, we can declare our testimony, "That He lives!"

MODIFICATIONS

Young children: No modifications needed.
Teens: No modifications needed.

FAMILY DISCUSSION STARTERS

Share your testimony of the Savior.

Now that you've shared with your family, what are ways you can share your testimony with others?

FAMILY HOME EVENING IDEAS

Song: "Silent Night," *Hymns,* 204.

Story: Discuss the story of the birth of Jesus in Luke 2.

Article: Study President Gordon B. Hinckley's article, "'To Do Good Always,'" *Ensign,* December 1994, 2–6.

Treat: Make candle cupcakes. Make and frost cupcakes. In the middle of each one, push in a rectangular caramel candy. Use a dab of frosting and attach a small red candy on the top like a flame.

Activity: As a family, attend a local "live" Nativity display. Or put together costumes and do your own acting out of the Nativity.

On Christmas night, start a Christmas stocking tradition. Our family has a small gold Christmas stocking that hangs on the mantle in our living room. On Christmas night, we gather as a family and write on a note card one gift we each would like to give to the Savior through the coming year. Gift ideas include "pray daily" or "read the Book of Mormon" or "be kind to my little brother all year." We date these notes and put them in the stocking; the stocking stays up all year as a reminder of our gift to the Savior. Throughout the year, we remind the family members to think about what they're working on.

Resource Guide

The following Web sites will provide valuable information in your quest to develop a culture of family service. Many of the sites pair volunteers with suitable projects. Others describe worthy charities and volunteer organizations that operate on both local and global levels.

You can also use your White or Yellow Pages to find volunteer opportunities. Look under "Volunteer," "Volunteer Center," "Social Services," or "Human Services."

1-800-VOLUNTEER

At http://www.1-800-volunteer.org, volunteers can search for volunteer opportunities. The site asks that you create a free account to use their services.

211.ORG

Dial 211 on your phone or go to www.211.org on the Internet to be connected to a large network of volunteer services.

AMERICAN RED CROSS

The American Red Cross is a relief organization guided by a United States Congressional Charter to bring relief to victims of disasters. In addition, the Red Cross works to help individuals, families, and communities prevent, prepare for, and respond to emergencies. Visit the Red Cross at http://www.redcross.org.

BOY SCOUTS OF AMERICA

The Boy Scouts mission statement is: "To prepare young people to make ethical and moral choices over their lifetimes by instilling in them the values of the Scout Oath and Law." There are many opportunities to volunteer and/or donate to the Boy Scouts. Visit the Boy Scouts on the Web at http://www.scouting.org.

BOYS & GIRLS CLUBS OF AMERICA

Boys & Girls Clubs offer positive experiences for boys and girls throughout America. BGCA provide safe havens for children who would otherwise be left alone during the hours before and after school and at other times of the week. Clubs also provide mentors, programs, and professional counselors to boys and girls in need. To learn more, visit http://www.bgca.org.

CARE

CARE works to educate individuals and communities throughout the world and provides opportunities to fight poverty, prevent the spread of HIV, bring clean water and food to needy communities, and help others recover from natural disasters. Visit http://www.care.org for more information.

CHARITY NAVIGATOR

Charity Navigator is an independent charity evaluator. Volunteers can use the Navigator to research everything from a charity's financial health to its nonprofit status. Log on to http://www.charitynavigator.org for more information.

THE CHURCH OF JESUS CHRIST OF LATTER-DAY SAINTS

The LDS Church's Humanitarian Services Center coordinates humanitarian relief projects around the globe. Service opportunities for members, families, friends of the Church, and others are many. Visit http://www.lds.org/humanitarianservices for more information.

To donate to one of the Church's programs, visit LDS Philanthropies at http://www.lds.org/ldsfoundation.

FAMILYCARES

The FamilyCares program is designed to help families find ways to serve together. Check them out at http://www.familycares.org.

GIRL SCOUTS OF THE USA

Girl Scouts of the USA provides numerous opportunities for millions of girls throughout the world. At their Web site, you can find opportunities to join in, volunteer, or donate to the Girl Scouts. Visit http://www.girlscouts.org.

GLOBAL VOLUNTEER NETWORK

The Global Volunteer Network offers volunteer opportunities throughout the world. Most opportunities involve travel to a community in need. For more information, visit http://www.volunteer.org.nz.

Resource Guide

HEIFER INTERNATIONAL

Heifer International seeks to end world poverty by helping volunteers make self-sustaining donations to communities in need. Volunteers can purchase cows, chickens, goats, pigs, and so on for donation to villages around the world. To learn more about this and Heifer's other initiatives, go to http://www.heifer.org.

KIDS CARE CLUBS

Kids Care Clubs allow school-aged children to capture the spirit of volunteerism. Visit their Web site at http://www.kidscare.org.

KIDS KORPS USA

Kids Korps USA works with Habitat for Humanity, Special Olympics, women's resource centers, homeless shelters, children's hospitals, senior centers, and environmental projects to provide service opportunities for children ages 5 to 18. Visit their Web site at http://www.kidskorps.org.

KIWANIS

Kiwanis Clubs throughout the world serve children and communities as they provide shelter, food, medical care, and mentorship to those in need. Learn more at http://www.kiwanis.org.

LIONS

Lions Clubs bring together volunteers who seek to give something back to their communities and improve the future of those who live within those communities. Visit the Lions Web site at http://www.lionsclubs.org.

MOTHERS WITHOUT BORDERS

Mothers Without Borders brings comfort, food, shelter, clothing, clean water, training, and other valuable opportunities to orphaned and vulnerable children in communities around the world. To learn more, visit http://www.motherswithoutborders.org.

PTA

The Parent-Teacher Association operates on local, statewide, and national levels to unite parents, teachers, and students at public schools throughout the country. Learn more at http://www.pta.org.

SOROPTIMIST

Soroptimist is an international volunteer organization for business and professional women. Their purpose is to make a difference in the lives of girls and women throughout the world. You can learn more at http://www.soroptimist.org.

ROTARY INTERNATIONAL

Rotary International describes itself as "a worldwide organization of business and professional leaders that provides humanitarian service, encourages high ethical standards in all vocations, and helps build good-will and peace in the world." To learn more, visit the Rotary Web site at http://www.rotary.org.

UNICEF

UNICEF, the United Nations Children's Fund, is mandated by the United Nations General Assembly. The group works to protect children's rights, decrease poverty, prevent the spread of HIV, immunize every child, and provide other basic needs to children in crisis. Learn more at http://www.unicef.org.

USA FREEDOM CORPS

USA Freedom Corps (USAFC) was created by President George W. Bush in 2002 as a national service initiative. At the USAFC Web site, volunteers can search for projects, connect with other volunteers, and learn more about a number of national service initiatives. Visit their Web site at http://www.usafreedomcorps.gov.

VOLUNTEERMATCH

VolunteerMatch matches volunteers with worthy projects in communities throughout the country. Simply log on to http://www.volunteermatch.org, enter your zip code, and browse the list of opportunities in your area.

References

CHAPTER HEADING QUOTATIONS FROM LATTER-DAY SAINT WRITERS AND LEADERS

Page 39: Gordon B. Hinckley, *Teachings of Gordon B. Hinckley,* 308.

Page 59: Henry B. Eyring, *To Draw Closer to God,* 88.

Page 72: Glenn L. Pace, "A Thousand Times," *Ensign,* November 1990, 9.

Page 84: "Clothed in Charity," *Ensign,* July 1999, 55.

Page 98: Gordon B. Hinckley, "Reaching Down to Lift Another," *Ensign,* November 2001, 54.

Page 102: Dallin H. Oaks, *Pure in Heart,* 37.

Page 104: Gordon B. Hinckley, "Look to the Future," *Ensign,* November 1997, 67.

Page 113: Thomas S. Monson, "Heavenly Homes, Forever Families," *Ensign,* June 2006, 103.

Page 116: Gordon B. Hinckley, "Living in the Fulness of Times," *Ensign,* November 2001, 6.

Page 119: Gordon B. Hinckley, "Forget Yourselves and Serve," *New Era,* July 2006, 5.

Page 128: Howard W. Hunter, in "We Must Stand Firm in the Faith," *Church News,* October 1, 1994.

Page 137: Marion D. Hanks, "The Royal Law of Love," *Ensign,* November 1988, 63.

Page 143: Marvin J. Ashton, "The Tongue Can Be a Sharp Sword," *Ensign,* May 1992, 19.

Page 151: Joseph B. Wirthlin, "Live in Thanksgiving Daily," *Ensign,* September 2001, 8.

Page 160: Susan Evans McCloud, "Lord, I Would Follow Thee," *Hymns,* no. 220.

Page 163: Anne C. Pingree, "Charity: One Family, One Home at a Time," *Ensign,* November 2002, 108.

Page 165: H. David Burton, "'Go, and Do Thou Likewise,'" *Ensign,* May 1997, 77.

Page 168: Ezra Taft Benson, "Godly Characteristics of the Master," *Ensign,* November 1986, 48.

Page 178: Dallin H. Oaks, "The Challenge to Become," *Ensign,* November 2000, 34.

Page 183: Robert J. Whetten, "True Followers," *Ensign,* May 1999, 30.

OTHER WORKS CITED

Children's Songbook. Salt Lake City: The Church of Jesus Christ of Latter-day Saints, 1997.

Eyring, Henry B. *To Draw Closer to God: A Collection of Discourses by Henry B. Eyring.* Salt Lake City: Deseret Book, 1997.

Hinckley, Gordon B. *Teachings of Gordon B. Hinckley.* Salt Lake City: Deseret Book, 1997.

References

Hymns of The Church of Jesus Christ of Latter-day Saints. Salt Lake City: Deseret Book, 1995.

McConkie, Bruce R. *The Mortal Messiah, Book 1: From Bethlehem to Calvary.* Salt Lake City: Deseret Book, 1979.

Oaks, Dallin H. *Pure in Heart.* Salt Lake City: Bookcraft, 1988.